The Spokesman

The carnage continues ... and now for Trident!

Edited by Ken Coates

Published by Spokesman for the
Bertrand Russell Peace Foundation

Spokesman 92   2006

CONTENTS

Editorial	3	*Ken Coates*
'No' in colour	8	*David Gentleman An Interview*
The Unseen Outrage	10	*John Berger, Noam Chomsky, Harold Pinter & José Saramago*
Apocalypse Near	11	*Noam Chomsky interviewed by Merav Yudilovitch*
Episode in the War Against Error	20	*Alexis Lykiard*
At a Crossroads	21	*Tadatoshi Akiba*
There Are No Safe Nukes	23	*Hans Blix*
Making Britain's Nukes 'Usable'?	30	*Paul Rogers*
Nuclear Dependency	39	*John Ainslie*
Fates Worse than DEATH	44	*Kurt Vonnegut*
Crisis of Greed	53	*Gabriel Kolko*
Whose Century?	60	*Immanuel Wallerstein*
Semper Fou	63	*James Alexander Thom*
Dossier	66	
Reviews	70	*Michael Barratt Brown J.E. Mortimer Christopher Gifford Roger Cole Tony Simpson*

Cover photo: Jess Hurd (reportdigital.co.uk)
Printed by the Russell Press Ltd., Nottingham, UK

ISSN 0262 7922   ISBN 0 85124 729 6

Subscriptions
Institutions £30 (UK)
                £35 (ex UK)
Individuals £20 (UK)
                £25 (ex UK)

Back issues available on request

A CIP catalogue record for this book is available from the British Library

Published by the
Bertrand Russell Peace Foundation Ltd.,
Russell House
Bulwell Lane
Nottingham NG6 0BT
England
Tel. 0115 9784504
email:
elfeuro@compuserve.com
www.spokesmanbooks.com
www.russfound.org

Editorial Board:
Michael Barratt Brown
Ken Coates
John Daniels
Ken Fleet
Stuart Holland
Tony Simpson

Routledge Classics

Get inside one of the greatest minds of the Twentieth Century

BERTRAND RUSSELL TITLES

History of Western Philosophy
Bertrand Russell

'Should never be out of print.'
– *The Evening Standard*

792pp: 0-415-32505-6: **£12.99**

Sceptical Essays
Bertrand Russell

With a new preface by **John Gray**

'Bertrand Russell wrote the best English prose of any twentieth-century philosopher.' – *The Times*

240pp: 0-415-32508-0: **£9.99**

In Praise of Idleness
Bertrand Russell

With a new introduction by **Anthony Gottlieb**

'There is not a page that does not provoke argument and thought.'
– *The Sunday Times*

192pp: 0-415-32506-4: **£8.99**

Why I Am Not a Christian
Bertrand Russell

With a new introduction by **Simon Blackburn**

'Devastating in its use of cold logic.'
– *The Independent*

272pp: 0-415-32510-2: **£9.99**

Power
Bertrand Russell

With a new introduction by **Samuel Brittan**

'Extremely penetrating analysis of human nature in politics.'
– *The Sunday Times*

288pp: 0-415-32507-2: **£9.99**

(New)

The Conquest of Happiness
Bertrand Russell

With a new preface by **A.C. Grayling**

'He writes what he calls common sense, but is in fact uncommon wisdom.'
– *The Observer*

200pp: 0-415-37847-8: **£9.99**

an **informa** business

www.routledge.com/classics

Available from all good bookshops

Editorial

The carnage continues ... and now for Trident!

Across Iraq, excluding Kurdistan, there were, in May 2006, 1,294 civilian deaths as a result of violence. The UN Assistance Mission reports that these people included 58 women and 17 children. Further, an additional 2,687 people were wounded, including 178 women and 41 children.

> 'In June 2006, 1554 civilians died violently (among them 66 women and 30 children). An additional 3,075 people were wounded ... The Medico Legal Institute (MLI) in Baghdad separately reported receiving 1,375 unidentified bodies in May, and 1,595 in June 2006. The total figure of civilians killed in Iraq adding the figures provided by the Ministry of Health and the MLI reaches 2,669 civilians in May and 3,149 in June 2006. According to the Ministry of Health, from January to June 2006 there were 6,826 civilians killed and 13,256 wounded. Including the figures of the MLI in Baghdad for the period, the total of civilians killed in Iraq from January to June 2006 was 13,338.'[1]

The Iraqi Ministry of Health acknowledged, on the 15th June 2006, that at least 50,000 persons have been violently killed since 2003. The Baghdad morgue alone has dealt with 30,204 bodies from 2003 to mid-2006.

The carnage has continued, and the month of July has seen a continuation of all these trends in mortality, registering, however, a modest increase. Some of these casualties were the unintended results of indiscriminate attacks, either bombings, or random shootings. People unhappily got in the way of other people's shoot-outs, sometimes involving the police or security forces, sometimes not. But other civilians died on purpose, in terrorist acts against targeted communities, or their Mosques or their markets.

Criminal violence also contributed to the tally. There are still executions, which have been reported not only from Baghdad, but also from Babil, Basra, Falluja, Karbala, Kirkuk, Mosel and Ramadi. Sometimes the bodies of those recovered show clear marks of torture. Sometimes buses or lorries are stopped, and those riding in them taken out and shot. In this context, the discussion about possible civil war, at some time in the future, must seem rather academic.

The slaughter in Iraq not only continues, but also continues to intensify. But the American and British forces do not appear to have any consistent strategy for diminishing this carnage in the areas over which they have asserted, by force of arms, the responsibility for law and order. Of order there is none, and of law only hollow words. True, the Americans have been compelled to dispatch additional forces, in numbers, to Baghdad. The British still focus their attention on withdrawal from suitable regions at some convenient time.

God knows the withdrawals are necessary, because there have during all this time been insane plans to maintain an expanded occupation in the Helmand province of Afghanistan. Collateral damage there has not yet begun to rival the death toll in Iraq, but the effort to prevent the return of the Taliban has already claimed over a hundred victims. The Taliban, of course, are already there.

4 The carnage continues ... and now for Trident!

As we go to press, the tenth British soldier has been killed in Helmand. He came from the Nottinghamshire mining village of Blidworth, and he was only 19. At the time that his embarkation was announced, the British Government claimed that he was expected to perform duties which would be calculated to win hearts and minds in Helmand, and assist in development work. It has since become abundantly plain that the then Defence Secretary John Reid's boast that he would be quite happy if the British force could complete three years service in Afghanistan without firing a shot was more Blairite deception, reached down from the same cupboard in which were kept all those mythical weapons of mass destruction.

Nato had been invited to send 9,000 additional troops to Afghanistan, raising the force total to 18,000. The requirement for these unlucky soldiers was advertised as a stabilisation and reconstruction effort. But the 3,000 British soldiers, like the rest of their Nato colleagues, found instead that they were expected to beat down a significant Taliban offensive, from which the American forces had wisely decided to disengage.

Poor relations, the British have arrived in Afghanistan in impractically small numbers, lamentably ill equipped. As the *Daily Mail* reported[2] early in the course of the exercise, the father of one of the first soldiers killed, an intelligence officer called Matthew Bacon, complained that his son

> "' had no protection at all from roadside bombs even though it was a known risk. If they had used properly armoured vehicles, British soldiers who have been killed in Iraq would have been alive today and Matthew may have been among them."
>
> The Snatch Land Rovers cost £50,000 while a more heavily armoured South African-made alternative considered by the MoD costs an estimated £20,000. Major Charles Heyman, editor of *Armed Forces of the United Kingdom*, said Britain is badly undermanned.
>
> "The problem we have is that we do not have enough fighting boots on the ground in Afghanistan. Just one third of our men are infantry. At any one time, of the 1,200 frontline troops, one third are sleeping and a third are either preparing for operations or coming back from operations. That means we effectively have just 400 troops in the field to control an area the size of Wales.
>
> There are more than 200 hardcore Taliban in the Sangin Valley and they have support through fear or favour from the population there. This is an area that has not been under Afghan Government control for years.'"[3]

Condoleezza Rice flew into Islamabad at this time, but not to bring comfort to the British soldiers. She was anxious to persuade Pakistan and Afghanistan to 'stop their bickering and work better together', but she was preoccupied with the need to step up the hunt for Osama Bin Laden. The *Daily Mail* wryly reported that Ms. Rice's visit

> 'comes at a time when both the Afghan and Pakistani leaders are suffering from slumps in popularity and their credibility is being questioned abroad'.

George W. Bush, of course, is hardly in a better situation.

President Karzai recently warned that it was time for the international community to rethink its strategy in Afghanistan 'because too many Afghans, including Taliban, were being killed'.

General James Jones heads the American and Nato forces in Europe, and has reportedly been urgently seeking to persuade the Nato allies to lift the restrictions they have imposed on the tasks assigned to their troops, which make it impossible for some of them to fight, or for commanders to co-ordinate a proper military campaign.

> '"What is the point of deploying troops who don't fight?" ask many Afghans. That is why General Jones calls these caveats – they now number a staggering 71 – "Nato's operational cancer".'

Ahmed Rashid reports that 'Nato's weaknesses are what worry President Hamid Karzai of the Afghan Government'. But if Nato may hope that these deficiencies are not noticed in its home countries, Karzai will be well aware that they are indeed noticed by the Taliban, who will appreciate the effect on public opinion of new body bags arriving across Europe.

New suicide bombers have appeared in the Afghan lands, where, earlier, they had never been seen.

After a four year span of diminishing authority in the country beyond the capital, President Karzai seems to have decided that his survival depends upon reaching an appropriate accommodation with the real men of influence in provincial Afghanistan. In a sharp appreciation of his position, Simon Jenkins reported in *The Guardian*[4] that Karzai, to survive

> 'must deal with existing power brokers, including the drug warlords – whatever this does for his reputation abroad. Last month he appalled western observers by appointing a dozen provincial police chiefs described to me by one UN official as "gangsters and criminals". Having failed to disarm local militias, he decided to pay them as regulars.'

Jenkins calculates that the British in Afghanistan are embarked upon mission impossible. John Reid, with his customary reticence, told Parliament that the effort to eliminate opium production was 'absolutely interlinked to the war on terror'. Jenkins points out that the Americans have turned a blind eye to this linkage, 'accepting that some eighty per cent of the country's exports by value are tied up in opium'. To eliminate the poppies and the Taliban together would, says Jenkins, need a Foreign Legion of 150,000 British troops in the desert. But there are only 6,000 of them.

The Dutch and the Canadian political leaders are, we are informed, very much averse to casualties among their soldiers which appears to imply that the British should be more profligate with the lives of the forces for which they have sole responsibility.

> 'Even the most starry-eyed neo-con could see little thanks in nation building in Kabul', says Jenkins. 'But the policy needed cover for its retreat. It needed a fall guy. Step forward plucky Britain, with Afghan glory lodged in its military genes.'

But the killing in the Middle East has reached its crescendo in the months of July and August, with the proxy war in the Lebanon. The proxy in question has been the state of Israel, which has levelled large parts of Lebanon, butchering something over one thousand of its Lebanese neighbours, in an effort, it claims, to destroy the Hezbollah resistance movement.

Like the thief who joins in the clamour of shouting 'Stop thief!', George Bush has accused Hezbollah of acting as proxies for Syria and Iran. Perhaps it is likely that Hezbollah has been able to arm itself with rockets and anti-tank weapons from Iran as well as Syria. But it is quite certain that Israel has been armed to the teeth by the United States, which has continued to ship planeloads of lethal weapons transiting through airports in the United Kingdom, to Israel. A horrid war has resulted, in which there have been considerably more than a thousand Lebanese civilian deaths, while the death toll in Israel has been numbered at one-tenth of that number, including the losses among combatants.

Seen as an ideological struggle, the neo-cons in the United States have described this as an effort by Hezbollah to 'establish a universal Islamist dictatorship'.

Le Monde Diplomatique quotes Michael Ledeen, of the American Enterprise Institute.

'It's war, and it now runs from Gaza into Israel, through Lebanon and thence to Iraq via Syria. There are different instruments, ranging from Hamas in Gaza to Hezbollah in Syria and Lebanon and on to the multifaceted insurgency in Iraq. But there is a common prime mover, and that is the Iranian mullahcracy, the revolutionary Islamic fascist state that declared war on us 27 years ago and has yet to be held accountable.'[5]

President Bush did not take long to parrot this outburst in denunciations of Islamic fascism. How long will it be before Mr. Blair also joins this chorus?

For the time being, Hezbollah have won in Lebanon, and Israel has been checked. Evidently this has been a reverse for the Anglo-American alliance, even if it may prove a temporary one.

With mayhem all around, will the Bush war machine launch itself into Iran? To Jack Straw, this seemed 'unthinkable'. But now surprise, surprise, Britain has a new Foreign Secretary. For all that, it still remains unthinkable that ground forces will be able to occupy Tehran. But it is, unfortunately, not at all unthinkable that air forces might visit the Iranians, even if it does appear likely that they may have no greater success than their Israeli proxies.

Surely, we live in difficult times.

* * *

Of course there is a marked shortage of sacrificial victims prepared to step forward and confront the wrath of the Jihad. Both in the United States and Britain, the recruitment campaigns of the military come up against lively and increasing difficulties. Worse, where they can, soldiers disengage. They are more and more reluctant to renew their contracts of service. The circumstance renders the decision to renew Trident, the British nuclear 'deterrent,' even more ominous than it was before. Like-minded Ministers have already uttered quite precise nuclear threats. Of course, this can be comfortably assumed to be merely bluster. But blustering when you are not at war is one thing: when your military forces are grossly over-stretched, and increasingly alienated, it is quite another.

The short truth is that there is no British Government, at present or in prospect, that can be trusted with the bomb. In the words of George W. Bush, it becomes more urgent than ever to put this wicked weapon beyond the reach of these wicked men.

Ken Coates

Footnotes
1. UN Assistance Mission for Iraq, *Human Rights Report*, 1st May to 30th June 2006.
2. David Williams and Tim Shipman, *Daily Mail*, 12th July 2006.
3. *Daily Mail*, 12th July 2006.
4. *The Guardian*, June 7th 2006.
5. *National Review Online*, 13th July 2006, cited in *Le Monde Diplomatique*, August 2006.

Blair not welcome in Beirut

'... Ghaleb Abu Zeynab, a member of Hezbollah's politburo, told *The Times* (24.08.06) that the people of Lebanon did not want Mr Blair's help. Speaking at an interview at Hezbollah headquarters in the southern suburbs of Beirut, he said: "Blair is not welcome in Lebanon. I am not speaking on behalf of Hezbollah but all the Lebanese people. They do not want someone who cried crocodile tears to visit their country. He is up to his ears in the blood of Lebanese women and children. He is not welcome here. He is a killer ..."'

'No' in colour

David Gentleman

An interview

David Gentleman, who created the Parliament Square installation which is featured on our cover, has been centrally involved in the protests in Britain against the war in Iraq. At the beginning of January, he gave an interview to the Socialist Worker, which we feature below, by kind permission. The questions are in italics, and David's replies in ordinary text.

Many people know you for your stamp designs. How did you first come to be involved in that?

I was invited out of the blue to take part in a limited competition to design a set of stamps for National Productivity Year, a very Stalinist-sounding subject. My designs combined a map of Britain with some energetic and productive-looking arrows.

Were you allowed to design in the way that you wanted or did you have to make changes? What sort of process was involved?

Only the subject was specified. How to tackle it was left to me. Once the design was accepted, I developed it to make it simpler and easier to print well.

I don't remember ever altering an idea, though I was once asked to. In the 1980s I designed some stamps for 'Ecology and the Environment'. It was at the time when people were beginning to get worried about threats to the environment, so it was an important subject. I produced a set of four designs showing the kind of creatures whose environment was under threat, such as fish from acid rain, symbolised by a power station cooling tower in the background. They were dramatic and easy to understand, and had an important message.

The Post Office's advisory committee liked them and proposed that they should go ahead. But before showing them to the queen for her approval, the Post Office also submitted them to Downing Street. This was during the Thatcher era, and the message came straight back that they must be made more 'industry-friendly'. I felt that toning down the message would have destroyed it, so the Post Office had to get somebody else to design the stamps.

You tried to take the queen's head off stamps. How did you go about that?

That's certainly what I had a shot at. In the mid-1960s, when Tony Benn became postmaster general, he asked anybody who was interested to write to him with suggestions for making stamps more interesting. I'd already designed a few sets of stamps, and I'd found out that stamps had very restricted subjects and that incorporating the queen's head on them meant cramming two conflicting kinds of image into a very small area. So, motivated by design considerations rather than by republicanism, I wrote to him saying that stamps would look better without the queen's head on them. Tony Benn then commissioned me to design an album of 100 stamp designs without the head, and took it to show the queen. The queen, or at any rate the palace, preferred the head to remain on the stamps, but accepted that it should become a small silhouette, which sat better alongside the real subject of the stamp. That's how it has appeared ever since.

Where can people find other examples of your work?

Londoners can find it on the Underground at Charing Cross on the Northern Line platforms, where my mural runs the length of a couple of platforms and shows the people who built the first Charing Cross and how they did it. I've also made a lot of lithographs, and I've written and illustrated half a dozen books about countries and cities. *David Gentleman's Britain* was the first. Others were about London, the Coastline, Paris, India, and Italy. The pictures were in watercolour, a medium I love for its freedom and practicality – it's the one I'm most at ease with. Last month I had a retrospective exhibition of watercolours at the Fine Art Society – 50 of them, one a year ever since I stopped being a student.

How did you get involved in designing for the Stop the War Coalition?

I started thinking about designing a protest poster when it was clear that Bush was preparing to attack Iraq and that Blair might let this country get dragged in. The best kinds of banners are the ones that people do themselves, because individually they have a wonderful creativity and anger about them. But I'd seen a photograph in the paper of a protest march with lots of people carrying banners. While it had a marvellous energy and vitality about it, it also looked a muddle, and you couldn't read the banners. I thought that if Stop the War Coalition were going to print their own posters, it would be worth making them as simple and as powerful as one could. My first design was a big, simple 'NO'. I stuck a lot of reduced copies of it over the press photo of the march to make a sea of 'NO's, and sent it to the Stop the War Coalition. That's probably what persuaded them to use it – it's certainly what the march looked like. Other designs followed for later marches.

How do you explain the contrast between your watercolours and these aggressive poster designs?

Even technically, they have more in common than you might think. The splashes of blood on the posters were made with watercolour, dropped onto handmade watercolour paper from about six feet high. But I've always been interested in ideas as well as appearances, and I don't think they're mutually exclusive.

The Unseen Outrage

John Berger
Noam Chomsky
Harold Pinter
José Saramago

The latest chapter of the conflict between Israel and Palestine began when Israeli forces abducted two civilians, a doctor and his brother, from Gaza. An incident scarcely reported anywhere, except in the Turkish press. The following day the Palestinians took an Israeli soldier prisoner – and proposed a negotiated exchange against prisoners taken by the Israelis – there are approximately 10,000 in Israeli jails.

That this 'kidnapping' was considered an outrage, whereas the illegal military occupation of the West Bank and the systematic appropriation of its natural resources – most particularly that of water – by the Israeli Defence (!) Forces is considered a regrettable but realistic fact of life, is typical of the double standards repeatedly employed by the West in face of what has befallen the Palestinians, on the land allotted to them by international agreements, during the last 70 years.

Today outrage follows outrage; makeshift missiles cross sophisticated ones. The latter usually find their target situated where the disinherited and crowded poor live, waiting for what was once called justice. Both categories of missile rip bodies apart horribly – who but field commanders can forget this for a moment?

Each provocation and counter-provocation is contested and preached over. But the subsequent arguments, accusations and vows, all serve as a distraction in order to divert world attention from a long-term military, economic and geographic practice whose political aim is nothing less than the liquidation of the Palestinian nation.

This has to be said loud and clear for the practice, only half declared and often covert, is advancing fast these days, and, in our opinion, it must be unceasingly and eternally recognised for what it is and resisted.

John Berger and Noam Chomsky are regular contributors to The Spokesman. *Harold Pinter and José Saramago were Nobel Prize Winners in 2005 and 1998 respectively.*

Apocalypse Near

Noam Chomsky
interviewed by
Merav Yudilovitch

Merav Yudilovitch is arts and culture reporter for Ynet, the English language version of Israel's largest daily newspaper Yediot Ahronot. Her questions and comments are printed in italic type, and Noam Chomsky's replies in ordinary type.

You say the provocation and counter-provocation all serve as a distraction from the real issue. Is the war in Lebanon also a distraction that aims to draw the world's attention to the north of Israel while Gaza is been destroyed?

I assume you are referring to John Berger's letter (see page 10). The 'real issue' that is being ignored is the systematic destruction of any prospects for a viable Palestinian existence as Israel annexes valuable land and major resources (water particularly), leaving the shrinking territories assigned to Palestinians as unviable cantons, largely separated from one another and from whatever little bit of Jerusalem is to be left to Palestinians, and completely imprisoned as Israel takes over the Jordan valley (and of course controls air space, etc.). This programme of '*hitkansut*', cynically disguised as 'withdrawal', is of course completely illegal, in violation of Security Council resolutions and the unanimous decision of the World Court (including the dissenting statement of US Justice Buergenthal). If it is implemented as planned, it spells the end of the very broad international consensus on a two-state settlement that the United States and Israel have unilaterally blocked for 30 years, matters that are so well documented that I do not have to review them here.

The United States and Israel do not tolerate any resistance to these plans, preferring to pretend, falsely of course, that 'there is no partner', as they proceed with programmes that go back a long way. We may recall that Gaza and the West Bank are recognised to be a unit, so that if resistance to Israel's destructive and illegal progammes is considered to be legitimate within the West Bank, then it is legitimate in Gaza as well, in reaction to Israeli actions in the West Bank.

To turn to your specific question, even a casual look at the Western press reveals that the crucial developments in the occupied territories are marginalised even more by the war in Lebanon. The ongoing destruction in Gaza, which was rarely seriously reported in the first place, has largely faded into the background, and the systematic takeover of the West Bank has virtually disappeared. The severe punishment of the population for 'voting the wrong way' was never considered problematic, consistent with the long-standing principle that democracy is fine if and only if it accords with strategic and economic interests, documented to the heavens. However, I would not go as far as the implication in your question that this was a purpose of the war, though it clearly is the effect.

Do you see the world media partially responsible for not insisting on linking what's going on in the occupied territories and Lebanon?

Yes, but that is the least of the charges that should be levelled against the world media, and the intellectual communities generally. One of many far more severe charges is brought up in the opening paragraph of the Berger letter. Recall the facts. On 25 June, Corporal Gilad Shalit was captured at an army post near Gaza, eliciting huge cries of outrage worldwide, continuing daily at a high pitch, and a sharp escalation in Israeli attacks in Gaza. The escalation was supported on the grounds that capture of a soldier is a grave crime for which the population must be punished. One day before, on 24 June, Israeli forces kidnapped two Gaza civilians, Osama and Mustafa Muamar, by any standards a far more severe crime than capture of a soldier. The Muamar kidnappings were certainly known to the major world media. They were reported at once in the English-language Israeli press (*Jerusalem Post*, *Ha'aretz* English edition, 25 June), basically Israeli Defence Force handouts. And there were indeed a few brief, scattered and dismissive reports in several newspapers around the United States; the only serious news report in English that day was in the Turkish press. Very revealingly, there was no comment, no follow-up, no call for military or terrorist attacks against Israel. A Google search will quickly reveal the relative significance in the West of the kidnapping of civilians by the Israeli Defence Force and the capture of an Israeli soldier a day later.

The paired events, a day apart, demonstrate with bitter clarity that the show of outrage over the Shalit kidnapping was cynical fraud. They reveal that by Western moral standards, kidnapping of civilians is just fine if it is done by 'our side', but capture of a soldier on 'our side' a day later is a despicable crime that requires severe punishment of the population. As Gideon Levy accurately wrote in *Ha'aretz*, the Israeli Defence Force kidnapping of civilians the day before the capture of Cpl. Shalit strips away any 'legitimate basis for the IDF's operation', and, we may add, any legitimate basis for support for these operations. The same assessment carries over to the July 12 kidnapping of two Israeli soldiers near the Lebanon border, heightened, in this case, by the (null) reaction to the regular Israeli practice for many years of abducting Lebanese and holding many as hostages for long periods, and of course killing many Lebanese. No one ever argued that these crimes justified bombing and shelling of Israel, invasion and destruction of much of the country, or terrorist actions within it. The conclusions are stark, clear, and entirely unambiguous.

All of this is, obviously, of extraordinary importance in the present case, particularly given the dramatic timing. That is, I suppose, why the major media chose to avoid the crucial facts, apart from a very few scattered and dismissive phrases.

Apologists for state crimes claim that the kidnapping of the Gaza civilians is justified by Israeli Defence Force claims that they are 'Hamas militants' or were planning crimes. By their logic, they should therefore be lauding the capture of Gilad Shalit, a soldier in an army that was (uncontroversially) shelling and bombing Gaza. These performances are truly disgraceful.

You're talking first and foremost about acknowledging the Palestinian nation but will it solve the 'Iranian threat', will it push the Hezbollah from the Israeli border? Today, Israelis see an immediate danger on the northern front. Are we being blinded?

Virtually all informed observers agree that a fair and equitable resolution of the plight of the Palestinians would considerably weaken the anger and hatred towards Israel and the United States in the Arab and Muslim worlds. Such an agreement is surely within reach, if the United States and Israel depart from their long-standing rejectionism. Before they were called off prematurely by Ehud Barak, the Taba negotiations of January 2001 were coming close to a viable settlement, carried forward by subsequent negotiations, most prominently the Geneva Accord released in December 2002, which received strong international support but was dismissed by the United States and rejected by Israel. One can raise various criticisms of these proposals, but they are at least a basis, perhaps a solid basis, for progress towards peaceful settlement if the United States and Israel sharply reverse their rejectionist policies.

On Iran and Hezbollah, there is, of course, much more to say, and I can only mention a few central points here.

Let us begin with Iran. In 2003, Iran offered to negotiate all outstanding issues with the United States, including nuclear issues and a two-state solution to the Israel-Palestine conflict. The offer was made by the moderate Khatami government, with the support of the hard-line 'supreme leader' Ayatollah Khamenei. The Bush administration response was to censure the Swiss diplomat who brought the offer.

In June 2006, Khamenei issued an official declaration stating that Iran agrees with the Arab countries on the issue of Palestine, meaning that it accepts the 2002 Arab League call for full normalisation of relations with Israel in a two-state settlement in accord with the international consensus. The timing suggests that this might have been a reprimand to his subordinate Ahmadinejad, whose inflammatory statements are given wide publicity in the West, unlike the far more important declaration by his superior Khamenei. Just a few days ago, former Iranian diplomat Saddagh Kharazzi 'reaffirmed that Iran would back a two-state solution if the Palestinians accepted' (*Financial Times*, 26 July 2006). Of course, the Palestine Liberation Organisation has officially backed a two-state solution for many years, and backed the 2002 Arab League proposal. Hamas has also indicated its willingness to negotiate a two-state settlement, as is surely well-known in Israel. Kharazzi is reported to be the author of the 2003 proposal of Khatami and Khamenei.

The United States and Israel do not want to hear any of this. They prefer to hear that Iran 'is sworn to the destruction of the Jewish state' (Jerusalem correspondent Charles Radin, *Boston Globe*, 2 August), the standard and more convenient story.

They also do not want to hear that Iran appears to be the only country to have accepted the proposal by International Atomic Energy Agency director Mohammed ElBaradei that all weapons-usable fissile materials be placed under international control, a step towards a verifiable Fissile Materials Cut-off Treaty (FMCT), as mandated by the UN General Assembly in 1993.

ElBaradei's proposal, if implemented, would not only end the Iranian nuclear crisis, but would also deal with a vastly more serious crisis: the growing threat of nuclear war, which leads prominent strategic analysts to warn of 'apocalypse soon' (Robert McNamara) if policies continue on their current course. The United States strongly opposes a verifiable Fissile Materials Cut-off Treaty, but over US objections, the treaty came to a vote at the United Nations, where it passed 147-1, with two abstentions: Israel, which cannot oppose its patron, and more interestingly, Blair's Britain, which retains a degree of sovereignty. The British ambassador stated that Britain supports the treaty, but it 'divides the international community' 147 to 1. These again are matters that are virtually suppressed outside of specialist circles, and are matters of literal survival of the species, extending far beyond Iran.

It is commonly said that the 'international community' has called on Iran to abandon its legal right to enrich uranium. That is true, if we define the 'international community' as Washington and whoever happens to go along with it. It is surely not true of the world. The non-aligned countries have forcefully endorsed Iran's 'inalienable right' to enrich uranium. And, rather remarkably, in Turkey, Pakistan, and Saudi Arabia, a majority of the population favour accepting a nuclear-armed Iran over any American military action, international polls reveal.

The non-aligned countries also called for a nuclear-free Middle East, a longstanding demand of the authentic international community, again blocked by the United States and Israel. It should be recognised that the threat of Israeli nuclear weapons is taken very seriously in the world. As explained by the former Commander-in-Chief of the US Strategic Command, General Lee Butler, 'it is dangerous in the extreme that in the cauldron of animosities that we call the Middle East, one nation has armed itself, ostensibly, with stockpiles of nuclear weapons, perhaps numbering in the hundreds, and that inspires other nations to do so'. Israel is doing itself no favours if it ignores these concerns.

It is also of some interest that when Iran was ruled by the tyrant installed by a US-UK military coup, the United States – including Rumsfeld, Cheney, Kissinger, Wolfowitz and others – strongly supported the Iranian nuclear programmes they now condemn and helped provide Iran with the means to pursue them. These facts are surely not lost on the Iranians, just as they have not forgotten the very strong support of the United States and its allies for Saddam Hussein during his murderous aggression, including help in developing the chemical weapons that helped kill hundreds of thousands of Iranians.

There is a great deal more to say, but it appears that the 'Iranian threat' to which you refer can be approached by peaceful means, if the United States and Israel would agree. We cannot know whether the Iranian proposals are serious, unless they are explored. The US-Israel refusal to explore them, and the silence of the United States (and, to my knowledge, European) media, suggests that it is perhaps feared that they may be serious.

I should add that to the outside world, it sounds a bit odd, to put it mildly, for the United Syates and Israel to be warning of the 'Iranian threat' when they and they alone are issuing threats to launch an attack, threats that are immediate and credible, and in serious violation of international law; and are preparing very openly for such an attack. Whatever one thinks of Iran, no such charge can be made in their case. It is also apparent to the world, if not to the United States and Israel, that Iran has not invaded any other countries, something that the United States and Israel have done regularly.

On Hezbollah too, there are hard and serious questions. As is well-known, Hezbollah was formed in reaction to the Israeli invasion of Lebanon in 1982 and its harsh and brutal occupation in violation of Security Council orders. Hezbollah won considerable prestige by playing the leading role in driving out the aggressors. Also, like other Islamic movements, including Hamas, it has gained popular support by providing social services to the poor. Along with Amal, now its close ally, Hezbollah represents the Shi'a community in the parliament in Lebanon's confessional system. It is an integral part of Lebanese society. And much as in the past, US-backed Israeli violence is sharply increasing popular support for Hezbollah, not only in the Arab and Muslim worlds generally, but also in Lebanon itself. Polls taken in late July reveal that 87 per cent of Lebanese support Hezbollah's fight with Israel, a rise of 29 per cent on a similar poll conducted in February. More striking, however, is the level of support for Hezbollah's resistance from non-Shiite communities. Eighty per cent of Christians polled supported Hezbollah along with 80 percent of Druze and 89 percent of Sunnis. 'Lebanese no longer blame Hezbollah for sparking the war by kidnapping the Israeli soldiers, but Israel and the United States instead' (Christian Science Monitor, 28 July 2006). As often in the past, Israel is doing itself no favours by failing to attend to the predictable consequences of its resort to extreme violence instead of such measures as prisoner exchange, as in the past.

It is also not wise to ignore the recent observations of Zeev Maoz (*Ha'aretz*, 24 July). As he wrote, the 'wall-to-wall consensus in Israel that the war against the Hezbollah in Lebanon is a just and moral war is based on selective and short-term memory, on an introverted world view, and on double standards'. The reasons include the Israeli practice of kidnapping and the almost daily violations of the

Lebanese border for surveillance: 'a border violation is a border violation'. The reasons also include the historical record: the four earlier Israeli invasions since 1978, and their grim consequences for Lebanese. And we should also not forget the pretexts. The 1982 invasion was carried out after a year in which Israel repeatedly carried out bombing and other provocations in Lebanon, apparently trying to elicit some PLO violation of the 1981 truce, and when it failed, attacked anyway, on the pretext of the assassination attempt against Ambassador Argov (by Abu Nidal, who was at war with the Palestine Liberation Organisation). The invasion was clearly intended, as virtually conceded, to end the embarrassing PLO initiatives for negotiation, a 'veritable catastrophe' for Israel as Yehoshua Porat pointed out. It was, as described at the time, a 'war for the West Bank'.

The later invasions also had shameful pretexts. In 1993, Hezbollah had violated 'the rules of the game', Yitzhak Rabin announced: these Israeli rules permitted Israel to carry out terrorist attacks north of its illegally-held 'security zone', but did not permit retaliation within Israel. Peres' 1996 invasion had no more credible pretexts. It is convenient to forget all of this, or to concoct tales about shelling of the Galilee in 1981, but it is not an attractive practice, nor a wise one.

The problem of Hezbollah's arms is quite serious, no doubt. Resolution 1559 calls for disarming of all Lebanese militias, but Lebanon has not enacted that provision. Sunni Prime Minister Fouad Siniora describes Hezbollah's military wing as 'resistance rather than as a militia, and thus exempt from' Resolution 1559. A National Dialogue in June 2006 failed to resolve the problem. Its main purpose was to formulate a 'national defence strategy' (*vis-à-vis* Israel), but it remained deadlocked over Hezbollah's call for 'a defense strategy that allowed the Islamic Resistance to keep its weapons as a deterrent to possible Israeli aggression' (Beirut-based journalist Jim Quilty, *Middle East Report*, July 25), in the absence of any credible alternative. The United States could, if it chose, provide a credible guarantee against an invasion by its client state, but that would require a sharp change in long-standing policy.

In the background are crucial facts emphasised by several veteran Middle East correspondents. Rami Khouri, an editor of Lebanon's *Daily Star*, writes that 'the Lebanese and Palestinians have responded to Israel's persistent and increasingly savage attacks against entire civilian populations by creating parallel or alternative leaderships that can protect them and deliver essential services'. Syria specialist Patrick Seale agrees: 'You have the rise of essentially non-state actors like Hezbollah and Hamas because of the vacuum created by the impotence of Arab states to contain or deter Israel. These actors are basically taking issue with Israel's "deterrence", which posits that Israel can strike but no one can strike at it'. Until such basic questions are dealt with, it is likely that 'the Middle East will sink further into violence and despair', as Khouri predicts.

You are not referring in your letter to the Israeli casualties. Is there differentiation in your opinion between Israeli casualties of war (and I'm not talking about soldiers, I'm talking about civilians) and Lebanese or Palestinian casualties?

That is not accurate. John Berger's letter is very explicit about making no distinction between Israeli and other casualties. As his letter states: 'Both categories of missile rip bodies apart horribly – who but field commanders can forget this for a moment'.

Why, in your opinion, is the world co-operating with the Israeli invasion of Lebanon, and why isn't there any real pressure on the Israeli government to stop the madness in Gaza and Jenin? What purpose does this silence serve?

The great majority of the world protests, but chooses not to act. Europe is unwilling to take a stand against the United States administration, which has made it clear that it supports Israeli policies in Palestine and Lebanon. The rest of the world strongly objects, but they are not even considered part of the 'international community', unless they obey. The US-backed Arab tyrannies at first condemned Hezbollah, but were forced to back down out of fear of their own populations. Even King Abdullah of Saudi Arabia, Washington's most loyal (and most important) ally, was compelled to say that 'If the peace option is rejected due to the Israeli arrogance, then only the war option remains, and no one knows the repercussions befalling the region, including wars and conflict that will spare no one, including those whose military power is now tempting them to play with fire'.

With regard to Palestine, while Bush's stand is extreme, it has its roots in earlier policies. The week in Taba in January 2001 is the only real break in US rejectionism in 30 years. During the Oslo years, the US-Israel hinted at joining the international consensus, but made sure it would be very difficult to implement by steady increase in settlement, the rate peaking in 2000. The United States also strongly supported earlier Israeli invasions of Lebanon, though, in 1982 and 1996, it compelled Israel to terminate its aggression when atrocities were reaching a point that harmed US interests.

Unfortunately, one can generalise a comment of Uri Avnery's about Dan Halutz, who 'views the world below through a bombsight'. Much the same is true of Rumsfeld-Cheney-Rice, and other top Bush administration planners, despite occasional soothing rhetoric. As history reveals, that view of the world is not uncommon among those who hold a virtual monopoly of the means of violence, with consequences that we need not review.

What is the next chapter in this Middle-Eastern conflict as you see it?

I do not know of anyone foolhardy enough to predict. The United States and Israel are stirring up popular forces that are very ominous, and which will only gain in power and become more extremist if the US and Israel persist in demolishing any hope of realisation of Palestinian national rights, and destroying Lebanon. It should also be recognised that Washington's primary concern, as in the past, is not Israel and Lebanon, but the vast energy resources of the Middle East, recognised

60 years ago to be a 'stupendous source of strategic power' and 'one of the greatest material prizes in world history'. We can expect, with confidence, that the United States will continue to do what it can to control this unparalleled source of strategic power. That may not be easy. The remarkable incompetence of Bush planners has created a catastrophe in Iraq, for their own interests as well. They are even facing the possibility of the ultimate nightmare: a loose Shi'a alliance (including Shi'ite-dominated Iraq, Iran, and the Shi'ite regions of Saudi Arabia), controlling the world's major energy supplies, and independent of Washington or even worse, establishing closer links with the China-based Asian Energy Security Grid and Shanghai Cooperation Council. The results could be truly apocalyptic. And even in tiny Lebanon, the leading Lebanese academic scholar of Hezbollah, and a harsh critic of the organisation, describes the current conflict in 'apocalyptic terms', warning that possibly 'All hell would be let loose' if the outcome of the US-Israel campaign leaves a situation in which 'the Shiite community is seething with resentment at Israel, the United States and the government that it perceives as its betrayer' (Amal Saad-Ghorayeb, *Washington Post*, 23 July).

It is no secret that in past years, Israel has helped to destroy secular Arab nationalism and to create Hezbollah and Hamas, just as US violence has expedited the rise of extremist Islamic fundamentalism and jihadi terror. The reasons are understood. There are constant warnings about it by Western (including US) intelligence agencies, and by the leading specialists on these topics. One can bury one's head in the sand and take comfort in a 'wall-to-wall consensus' that what we do is 'just and moral' (Maoz), ignoring the lessons of recent history, or simple rationality. Or one can face the facts, and approach dilemmas which are very serious by peaceful means. They are available. Their success can never be guaranteed. But we can be reasonably confident that viewing the world through a bombsight will bring further misery and suffering, perhaps even 'apocalypse soon'.

Reproduction of the article was authorised by ynet. All the rights are reserved to ynet (www.ynetnews.com).

Bakers, Food & Allied Workers Union

*Suuporting workers in struggle
Wherever they may be.*

Joe Marino   General Secretary
Ronnie Draper   President
Jackie Mander   Vice President

Stanborough House,
Great North Road,
Stanborough,
Welwyn Garden City,
Hertfordshire. AL8 7TA
Phone 01707 260150& 01707 259450
www.bfawu.org

Episode in the War Against Error
[Stockwell tube station, London, 21 July 2005]
by Alexis Lykiard

Hired guns hunted down one ... Brazilian,
young naïf coldly rendered to death.
They collared the sinister Alien,
who gave up, underground, his last breath.
It seems he was seated – no hurry at first.
Did the marksmen yell boldly, as they'd rehearsed,
and pin flat the accused or rather, Accursed?
The name of this fair game is Kill-not-cure,
codenames and no packdrill, its aim unsure:
targets exist to be hit with each burst.
While passengers freeze, turn sideways in dread,
seven bullets point-blank blow open his head.

* * *

Note: An eighth bullet hit 27-year-old Jean Charles de Menezes in the shoulder. Three more shots missed. The Daily Telegraph *later announced on its front page (16/11/05) that hollow-point – or dum-dum-ammunition, 'banned in warfare under international convention' – was used.*

At a Crossroads

Tadatoshi Akiba

Tadatoshi Akiba is the mayor of Hiroshima, who issued this Declaration on behalf of the city as an appeal to the world on Hiroshima Day, 6 August 2006.

Radiation, heat, blast and their synergetic effects created a hell on Earth. Sixty-one years later, the number of nations enamoured of evil and enslaved by nuclear weapons is increasing. The human family stands at a crossroads. Will all nations be enslaved? Or will all nations be liberated? This choice poses another question. Is it acceptable for cities, and especially the innocent children who live in them, to be targeted by nuclear weapons?

The answer is crystal clear, and the past sixty-one years have shown us the path to liberation.

From a hell in which no one could have blamed them for choosing death, the *hibakusha* set forth towards life and the future. Living with injuries and illnesses eating away at body and mind, they have spoken persistently about their experiences. Refusing to bow before discrimination, slander, and scorn, they have warned continuously that 'no one else should ever suffer as we did'. Their voices, picked up by people of conscience the world over, are becoming a powerful mass chorus.

The keynote is, 'The only role for nuclear weapons is to be abolished'. And yet, the world's political leaders continue to ignore these voices. The International Court of Justice advisory opinion handed down ten years ago, born of the creative action of global civil society, should have been a highly effective tool for enlightening and guiding them towards the truth.

The Court found that '… the threat or use of nuclear weapons would generally be contrary to the rules of international law', and went on to declare,

'There exists an obligation to pursue in good faith and bring to a conclusion negotiations leading to nuclear disarmament in all its aspects under strict and effective international control.'

If the nuclear-weapon states had taken the lead and sought in good faith to fulfil this obligation, nuclear weapons would have been abolished already. Unfortunately, during the past ten years, most nations and most people have failed to confront this obligation head-on. Regretting that we have not done more, the City of Hiroshima, along with Mayors for Peace, whose member cities have increased to 1,403, is launching Phase II of our *2020 Vision Campaign*. This phase includes the *Good Faith Challenge*, a campaign to promote the good-faith negotiations for nuclear disarmament called for in the ICJ advisory opinion, and a *Cities Are Not Targets* project demanding that nuclear-weapon states stop targeting cities for nuclear attack.

Nuclear weapons are illegal, immoral weapons designed to obliterate cities. Our goals are to reveal the delusions behind 'nuclear deterrence theory' and the 'nuclear umbrella', which hold cities hostage, and to protect, from a legal and moral standpoint, our citizens' right to life.

Taking the lead in this effort is the United States Conference of Mayors, representing 1,139 American cities. At its national meeting this past June, the Conference adopted a resolution demanding that all nuclear-weapon states, including the United States, immediately cease all targeting of cities with nuclear weapons.

Cities and citizens of the world have a duty to release the lost sheep from the spell and liberate the world from nuclear weapons. The time has come for all of us to awaken and arise with a will that can penetrate rock and a passion that burns like fire.

I call on the Japanese government to advocate for the *hibakusha* and all citizens by conducting a global campaign that will forcefully insist that the nuclear-weapon states 'negotiate in good faith for nuclear disarmament'. To that end, I demand that the government respect the Peace Constitution of which we should be proud. I further request more generous, people-oriented assistance appropriate to the actual situations of the ageing *hibakusha*, including those living overseas and those exposed in 'black rain areas'.

To console the many victims whose names remain unknown, this year for the first time we added the words 'Many Unknown' to the ledger of victims' names placed in the cenotaph. We humbly pray for the peaceful repose of the souls of all atomic bomb victims and a future of peace and harmony for the human family.

There are no safe nukes

Hans Blix

An excerpt from the Blix Report

In September 2003, Swedish Foreign Minister Anna Lindh informed the Russell Foundation of her Government's plans to sponsor an independent, international commission 'to stimulate new thinking and to offer new ideas on how to pursue disarmament and non-proliferation of weapons of mass destruction' (see Dealing with the Hydra: Proliferation and Full Spectrum Dominance *by Ken Coates). Several days later, she was murdered while shopping in Stockholm.*

These excerpts on nuclear weapons are taken from chapter three of the ensuing report on Weapons of Terror, *chaired by Dr Hans Blix, formerly the United Nations' chief weapons inspector. The full report and the Commission's detailed recommendations are available online (www.wmdcommission.org).*

So long as any state has nuclear weapons, others will want them. So long as any such weapons remain, there is a risk that they will one day be used, by design or accident. And any such use would be catastrophic.

The accumulated threat posed by the estimated 27,000 nuclear weapons, in Russia, the United States and the other Non-Proliferation Treaty nuclear-weapon states, merits worldwide concern. However, especially in these five states the view is common that nuclear weapons from the first wave of proliferation somehow are tolerable, while such weapons in the hands of additional states are viewed as dangerous.

In this view, the second wave of proliferation, which added Israel, India and Pakistan, was unwelcome – the lack of political stability in Pakistan being a special source of concern. However, efforts to induce these states to roll back their programmes – as South Africa did – have gradually been weakened and are now largely abandoned. As none of them was a party to the Non-Proliferation Treaty, they could not be charged with a violation of the Treaty.

The third wave of proliferation, consisting of Iraq, Libya, North Korea and possibly Iran, is seen as a mortal danger and has met with a much more forceful reaction.

The Commission rejects the suggestion that nuclear weapons in the hands of some pose no threat, while in the hands of others they place the world in mortal jeopardy. Governments possessing nuclear weapons can act responsibly or recklessly. Governments may also change over time. Twenty-seven thousand nuclear weapons are not an abstract theory. They exist in today's world. The Hiroshima and Nagasaki bombs, each of which had an explosive yield of less than 20 kilotons of TNT, killed some 200,000 people. The W-76 – the standard nuclear warhead used on US Trident submarine-launched ballistic missiles – has a yield of up to 100 kilotons. During the Cold War, the Soviet Union manufactured and tested nuclear weapons with yields of over 50 megatons of TNT.

The questions of how to reduce the threat and the number of existing nuclear weapons must be addressed with no less vigour than the question of the threat from additional weapons, whether in the hands of existing nuclear-weapon states, proliferating states or terrorists.

It is probably true that an agreement by all nuclear-armed states to, say, a fissile material cut-off would not in itself prevent the proliferation threat posed by North Korea or Iran. Nevertheless, dissuading potential proliferators from moving further along the path of nuclear-weapon development, and maintaining support by the global community for non-proliferation, is made more difficult when the nuclear-weapon states make little effort to achieve nuclear disarmament. Explanations by the nuclear-haves that the weapons are indispensable to defend their sovereignty are not the best way to convince other sovereign states to renounce the option. The single most hopeful step to revitalize non-proliferation and disarmament today would be ratification of the Comprehensive Test Ban Treaty by all states that have nuclear weapons.

As was seen in 2005, both at the NPT Review Conference and at the United Nations World Summit, the world community will not agree to choose between non-proliferation and disarmament. This chapter advances recommendations on both fronts.

Over the six decades following the attacks on Hiroshima and Nagasaki, numerous initiatives have been launched to control and eliminate nuclear weapons and to prevent proliferation. They have had mixed results. Seen from one perspective, the efforts have failed. At least eight and possibly nine states have acquired nuclear weapons. Global stocks of these weapons are still huge, and

Some progress in reducing nuclear threats

- The non-use of nuclear weapons since 1945 shows that there is a significant threshold against use.
- Nearly all states in the world have adhered to the NPT, including four states that have been in possession of nuclear weapons – South Africa and three former members of the Soviet Union. With a few notable exceptions the parties are abiding by their commitment not to acquire nuclear weapons.
- Regional nuclear-weapon-free zones have made virtually the entire southern hemisphere off-limits for the stationing of nuclear weapons. Other treaties outlaw basing such weapons on the seabed, in outer space and in Antarctica.
- The Partial Test-Ban Treaty bans nuclear testing everywhere except underground. While the Comprehensive Nuclear-Test-Ban Treaty has not entered into force, a moratorium against testing is being upheld.
- The US and Russia have withdrawn thousands of nuclear weapons from service. The UK has significantly reduced its arsenal after the end of the Cold War, while France no longer deploys nuclear weapons on surface-to-surface missiles or as gravity bombs.

more states and even terrorists might acquire them. But against this there have been some positive achievements (see Box).

The three major challenges the world confronts – existing weapons, further proliferation and terrorism – are interlinked politically, and also practically: the larger the existing stocks, the greater the danger of leakage and misuse. This chapter begins by addressing the proliferation issue because it has been at the forefront of international debate and action in recent years. But the Commission takes all three challenges equally seriously. Progress and innovative solutions are needed on all fronts.

Preventing the proliferation of nuclear weapons

The Non-Proliferation Treaty
Having entered into force in 1970, the treaty is the cornerstone of the global non-proliferation regime. The original 'bargain' of the treaty is generally understood to be the elimination of nuclear weapons through the commitment by non-nuclear-weapon states not to acquire nuclear weapons and the commitment by five nuclear-weapon states to pursue nuclear disarmament. In addition, the treaty requires parties to facilitate peaceful uses of nuclear energy through exchanges of various kinds between themselves. They also promise to enter into safeguards agreements with the International Atomic Energy Agency and to exercise control over their national nuclear-related exports. Only four countries in the world (India, Israel, North Korea and Pakistan) are not parties to the treaty. What accounts for this near universality?

Many states did not perceive a need for nuclear weapons of their own. Some had assurances of protection through their alliances and other arrangements. Some may well have responded to political and diplomatic pressure to renounce nuclear weapons, while others may not have had a technical capability to develop them. Yet others, even if they could have made a nuclear weapon, have abhorred such weapons and wanted to join a treaty that could be an obstacle to the continued possession of the deadliest weapon in history.

Conversely, when states have perceived threats to their security (like India, Israel, Pakistan and South Africa) or have felt ostracized and at risk (like North Korea, Libya and Iran), this may have weighed heavily in their calculations. In Iraq's case, by contrast, Saddam Hussein's efforts to develop nuclear weapons may have been motivated more by a wish to dominate and expand Iraq's influence in the region than by concerns about national security.

The two basic ideas at the heart of the Non-Proliferation Treaty continue to have strong international support – that more fingers on more nuclear triggers would result in a more dangerous world, and that non-proliferation by the have-nots and disarmament by the haves will together lead to a safer world. Nevertheless, the fact that the treaty is facing several problems must be squarely faced.

The first problem relates to the *failure to make progress towards nuclear disarmament* by the nuclear-weapon states parties.

The second set of problems concerns the *breaches of the treaty or of International Atomic Energy Agency safeguards obligations* by a small number of parties: Iraq,

Libya, North Korea and Iran. Their actions have undermined the confidence in the Non-Proliferation Treaty. A domino effect, it has been suggested, may lead more countries to acquire nuclear weapons. However, while it is necessary to examine the fundamental questions of verification, compliance, reliability and enforcement, one must note that the world is not replete with would-be proliferators nor, as yet, with nuclear-capable terrorists. As long as relations between the great powers are characterized by cooperation and regional tensions are not heightened, there is probably little reason to fear a collapse of the Non-Proliferation Treaty.

A third problem, related to the second and illustrated by the case of North Korea, is that the treaty's provision regarding *withdrawal* fails to identify such action as the serious event it is. It makes it simply procedural. Any notice of withdrawal must be brought to the attention of all other states parties and the UN Security Council, which will examine whether the planned withdrawal constitutes a threat to the peace and consider what measures it might take. If the Security Council fails to respond to a withdrawal, other parties might later decide to reconsider their own continued adherence to the treaty.

A fourth problem may be characterized as *technical*. The lack of any provision for a standing secretariat to assist the parties in implementing the treaty has proven inconvenient.

In fact, the Non-Proliferation Treaty is the weakest of the treaties on weapons of mass destruction in terms of provisions about implementation. The International Atomic Energy Agency and its Board of Governors are not the secretariat of the treaty, and the three depositary governments – the Russian, the British and the United States – have only been given the formal task of convoking review conferences. The NPT has no provisions for consultations or special meetings of the parties to consider cases of possible non-compliance or withdrawal, nor to assist in the implementation of the treaty between the five-yearly Review Conferences. The governments of Canada, Ireland and many other states have offered constructive proposals to address this institutional deficit, with options that include creating a standing bureau or executive committee of the parties. Yet the problem persists, and the periodic meetings of the treaty review process cannot offer an effective substitute for this needed institutional reform.

The problems described above do not diminish the fundamental support for the treaty but there is unquestionably a serious malaise among parties, as shown in their inability to adopt any common conclusions at the 2005 Review Conference.

The hope and expectation have faded – at least for now – that the basic bargain of the treaty between nuclear-weapon and non-nuclear-weapon states should lead to parallel and mutually reinforcing processes of non-proliferation and disarmament. There is a background to this concern.

Evolving treaty commitments
The negotiation of the Non-Proliferation Treaty in the late 1960s was not as easy as might be assumed. Several non-nuclear-weapon states were critical of the imbalance between the precise obligations of the non-nuclear-weapon states and

the imprecise commitments of the nuclear powers. One result was a provision stating that the treaty would remain in force for only 25 years, requiring a subsequent decision on an extension.

During the 1970s and 1980s, the failure of the nuclear-weapon states to make progress on disarmament and to halt nuclear testing led to growing criticism from the non-nuclear-weapon states. Many states, not only in the Middle East, voiced their concern that Israel remained outside the treaty while other states in the region were subject to NPT constraints. The indefinite extension of the NPT in 1995 was not a forgone conclusion.

While the parties ultimately agreed in 1995, after intensive negotiations, to extend the treaty indefinitely, this decision was adopted only as part of a package of commitments. This included a decision on principles and objectives for non-proliferation and disarmament, a decision on strengthening the treaty review process and a resolution on the establishment of a weapons of mass destruction-free zone in the Middle East. The disarmament goals called for completion of a comprehensive test ban treaty, negotiations on a verifiable fissile material cut-off treaty, and further systematic progress on reducing and eliminating nuclear weapons. The parties showed that it was possible to reconcile their strong and diverse individual interests.

The treaty's 2000 Review Conference carried on this process of multilateral cooperation. It agreed on a Final Document that included 'the thirteen practical steps' for further progress towards nuclear disarmament. These were seen as representing a continuation and development of the agreements that had secured the indefinite extension of the Non-Proliferation Treaty five years earlier.

At the 2005 Review Conference this cooperative approach was missing. The conference ended in acrimony and without any final statement. 'The thirteen practical steps' were played down by the nuclear-weapon states and not recognized as important commitments. The inability of the World Summit in September 2005 to adopt any statement about disarmament and non-proliferation was caused by a renewed failure to balance commitments in the two areas. The obvious question therefore is: what can be done to revitalize the Non-Proliferation Treaty?

Commission Recommendations

- All parties to the Non-Proliferation Treaty need to revert to the fundamental and balanced non-proliferation and disarmament commitments that were made under the treaty and confirmed in 1995 when the treaty was extended indefinitely.
- All parties to the Non-Proliferation Treaty should implement the decision on principles and objectives for non-proliferation and disarmament, the decision on strengthening the Non-Proliferation Treaty review process, and the resolution on the Middle East as a zone free of nuclear and all other weapons of mass destruction, all adopted in 1995. They should also promote the implementation of 'the thirteen practical steps' for nuclear disarmament that were adopted in 2000.

- To enhance the effectiveness of the nuclear non-proliferation regime, all Non-Proliferation Treaty non-nuclear-weapon states parties should accept comprehensive safeguards as strengthened by the International Atomic Energy Agency Additional Protocol.

The states parties to the Non-Proliferation Treaty should establish a standing secretariat to handle administrative matters for the parties to the treaty. This secretariat should organize the treaty's Review Conferences and their Preparatory Committee sessions. It should also organize other treaty-related meetings upon the request of a majority of the states parties.

* * *

Nuclear-weapon-free zones

In the late 1940s and 1950s, the failure to outlaw nuclear weapons led some governments to look for intermediate steps towards that goal. One such initiative was to ban the stationing, testing, use or development of nuclear weapons in certain geographic areas – nuclear-weapon-free zones. Early efforts focused on unpopulated areas or environments, resulting in treaties covering Antarctica, the seabed and outer space.

The Tlatelolco Treaty, signed in 1967, broke new ground by seeking to include within the designated zone the entire populated region of Latin America and the Caribbean. The Treaties of Rarotonga (1986), Pelindaba (1996) and Bangkok (1997) created nuclear-weapon-free zones in the South Pacific, Africa, and Southeast Asia. Also, five former Soviet republics have provisionally agreed upon the text of a treaty to establish a nuclear-weapon-free-zone in Central Asia. The concept of nuclear-weapon-free zones has emerged as a success story.

Nuclear-weapon-free zones serve some important functions. They fill the gap in the NPT that allowed the foreign deployment of nuclear weapons on the territory of non-nuclear-weapon states – no such weapons may be stationed in the zones. They complement and reinforce the basic non-proliferation commitments of the NPT. Through protocols to the treaties creating such zones, the nuclear-weapon states can provide legally binding negative security assurances to members of such regimes. They also contribute to the strengthening of comprehensive ('full-scope') IAEA safeguards, by requiring the domestic application and/or requirement of such safeguards for exports leaving the region. Furthermore, they help to strengthen the global norm against nuclear testing, pending entry into force of the Comprehensive Test Ban Treaty.

These regimes, however, face many challenges. For instance, the Pelindaba Treaty, although almost a decade old, has still not entered into force. Of all the protocols to the nuclear-weapon-free zone treaties, only the relevant protocol to the Tlatelolco Treaty has been ratified by all five nuclear-weapon states. None of the nuclear-weapon states has ratified the protocol to the Bangkok Treaty, although China has said that it may agree to it independently of the other nuclear-weapon states.

In addition, many states in the zones have failed to conclude their required full-scope safeguards agreements with the International Atomic Energy Agency. And while all the treaties creating such zones are of indefinite duration, they all contain withdrawal clauses. This opens questions about the reversibility of the commitments made.

Commission Recommendation

- All Non-Proliferation Treaty nuclear-weapon states that have not yet done so should ratify the protocols of the treaties creating regional nuclear-weapon-free zones. All states in such zones should conclude their comprehensive safeguards agreements with the International Atomic Energy Agency and agree to ratify and implement the Additional Protocol.

Making Britain's nukes 'usable'?

Paul Rogers

Paul Rogers is Professor of Peace Studies at the University of Bradford. A collection of his briefings for the Oxford Research Group, Iraq and the War on Terror: Twelve Months of Insurgency, 2004-05, *is published by IB Tauris.*

In just five words, Gordon Brown, the United Kingdom's Chancellor of the Exchequer and would-be successor to Tony Blair, has intentionally reignited the debate over the future of Britain's nuclear weapons. In a wide-ranging speech on 21 June 2006 focusing on global markets, financial services and economic policy, he included as part of his prognosis for UK security in the 21st century the commitment to 'retaining our independent nuclear deterrent'.

As so often with New Labour, the way the entire speech was 'spun' by Brown's aides was revealing. This element was, they indicated, key among all the topics the Chancellor covered. As Andrew Rawnsley commented:

> 'It has enraged the Left of the Labour Party. It was contrived to do just that. It was unashamedly designed – Mr Brown's acolytes make no pretence otherwise – to try to make the Chancellor a more appealing figure to Middle England.' (see 'Why Gordon Brown decided to go nuclear', *Observer*, 25 June 2006).

In the coming weeks and months there may well be a debate on plans to replace Trident – Britain's submarine-launched ballistic nuclear-weapons system – and it is probable that Labour will, in due course, make its decision. There could be some discussion in Parliament and there might even be a vote, though few doubt the outcome. 'Middle England' will no doubt remain comforted by Britain preserving its civilised, semi-great-power status by retaining the capacity to kill tens of millions of people. The wider point, though, is that there is a vigorous attempt to confine the debate to the limited theme of a 'deterrent'. Indeed, the entire debate is constructed along the very narrow premise that Britain's nuclear weapons offer, and have always offered, nothing more than a last-ditch deterrent protection against a would-be enemy threatening the country with annihilation.

During the forty-five-year Cold War, that

enemy was seen to be the Soviet Union. This now presents some difficulties in that the much-missed 'evil empire' has disappeared, removing the original point of possessing the bomb. It isn't clear, for example, how Trident could have prevented the London bombings of 7 July 2005. After all, nuking the home towns of the young bombers – Leeds and Dewsbury – in retaliation would have been a bit excessive, even for New Labour. Still, George W Bush has neatly constructed an 'axis of evil' to replace the late, lamented Soviet Union. This offers his closest ally Tony Blair (and his successor as British Prime Minister) the opportunity to argue that Trident's successor is designed to deter threats from those Islamofascists in Tehran, the world-conquering James Bond-hating hordes of North Korea, the Taliban when they take over Pakistan, the Naxalites when New Delhi finally falls and, of course, that historic enemy – the French.

Every part of this construct, however, is still underpinned by the doctrine of 'deterrence'. Middle England must rest secure in the knowledge that our nuclear weapons are 'good' nuclear weapons and would only ever be used as weapons of final response – after, perhaps, not just Middle England but also the furthest bits of Wales, Scotland and even Northern Ireland had been turned to radioactive dust.

The problem with this is that it is one of the great myths of the nuclear age. Ever since the atom bombs on Hiroshima and Nagasaki performed the same destructive tasks that had previously required thousand-bomber raids (such as the devastating fire-bombing of Tokyo), the nuclear age has been replete with the idea that nuclear weapons are usable as weapons of war. This has been central to the North Atlantic Treaty Organisation (Nato's) nuclear planning, as well as to the Warsaw Pact (and now Russia).

Nato as an alliance, and Britain as a state, have long planned to fight nuclear wars at levels falling far short of a cataclysmic central nuclear exchange. This also means that Nato and Britain have had, and still maintain, policies that can envisage 'first use' of nuclear weapons.

On the eve of what could possibly be a period of open debate about the role of Britain's nuclear weapons, it might be useful to trace this somewhat hidden history. This could serve the purpose of revealing matters that successive governments prefer to avoid discussing in public, and thus help ensure a more interesting debate.

This debate must consider two distinct issues: Nato as an alliance of which Britain is a prominent member, and Britain's long-term pursuit of policies for nuclear first use outside the Nato area.

The early days

Britain commenced its nuclear-weapons programme shortly after the end of the Second World War. It tested a fission (atomic) bomb in October 1952 and a crude fusion (hydrogen) bomb in May 1957. By the end of the 1950s, Britain had developed a strategic nuclear force based on the V-bomber medium-range jet bombers: the Valiant, Victor and Vulcan.

From the mid-1960s, Britain began to develop a force of ballistic-missile submarines capable of deploying the United States' Polaris submarine-launched ballistic missile (SLBM). The first such submarine, *Resolution*, started to patrol in June 1968, and control of the UK strategic nuclear force passed to the Royal Navy in July 1969.

Britain also developed a range of tactical nuclear weapons, principally bombs, deployed on a number of land-based and carrier-based strike aircraft from the late-1950s onwards. These included the Scimitar, Buccaneer, Jaguar and Sea Harrier, and the Lynx and Sea King helicopters. In addition, US-made nuclear depth-bombs were carried by Nimrod maritime-patrol aircraft; and Lance missiles and self-propelled artillery carrying US-made nuclear warheads were deployed with the British Army in West Germany. At its peak, in the early 1980s, Britain deployed some 400 of its own nuclear weapons together with several scores of US nuclear weapons. With the ending of the Cold War, most of the types of nuclear weapons declined fairly rapidly, but two major types of British nuclear weapon remained in service until the late 1990s: the Polaris submarine-launched ballistic missile and the WE-177 tactical nuclear bomb.

In the 1990s, these were replaced by Trident, another submarine-launched missile. This is deployed with two warheads, a powerful strategic warhead many times more destructive than the Hiroshima bomb, and a 'sub-strategic' or tactical warhead that has around half the explosive power of the Hiroshima bomb.

Since the 1950s onwards, Britain has operated a twin-track policy of committing nuclear forces to Nato and having them available for independent deployment and possible use.

Nato's nuclear planning

Although the early nuclear weapons of the 1940s and early 1950s were essentially strategic – intended for use against the core assets of an opposing state – the development of nuclear weapons intended for tactical use within particular war-zones was an early feature of the east-west nuclear confrontation. By the late 1950s, both the United States and the Soviet Union were developing relatively low-yield freefall bombs as well as early forms of nuclear-capable artillery. Over the next twenty-five years, a remarkable array of tactical nuclear weapons was developed and deployed, covering almost every type of military posture.

As well as freefall bombs, short-range battlefield missiles were developed along with nuclear-tipped anti-aircraft missiles and several types of nuclear artillery and mortars. Nuclear landmines known as atomic demolition munitions were developed that could be emplaced to destroy major bridges or tunnels or even block mountain passes. At sea, submarines were equipped with nuclear-tipped torpedoes, surface ships carried anti-submarine nuclear depth-bombs which could be delivered by missile or helicopter, and aircraft carriers could fly off strike aircraft carrying several kinds of nuclear bomb. There were even air-to-air missiles such as the US Genie, that were nuclear-armed.

By the 1980s, there were around 20,000 tactical nuclear weapons deployed by the United States and the Soviet Union, based in more than fifteen countries and on warships and submarines throughout the world. In the great majority of cases, the presumption was that if such weapons were used, they would not necessarily involve an escalation to an all-out nuclear war. In other words, nuclear warfighting could be controlled. In Europe, perhaps the tensest region of the Cold War nuclear confrontation, both alliances had policies of the first use of nuclear weapons in response to conventional attack. (For a full discussion, see the relevant chapter, 'Learning from the Cold War', in Paul Rogers, *Losing Control: Global Security in the 21st Century*, Pluto Press, 2002).

For Nato in the 1950s, before the Soviet Union had developed a large arsenal of nuclear weapons, the posture was codified in a military document MC14/2, colloquially termed the 'tripwire' posture. Any Soviet attack against Nato would be met with a massive nuclear retaliation, including the use of US strategic nuclear forces; this assumed that the US could destroy the Soviet Union's nuclear forces and its wider military potential without suffering unacceptable damage itself.

By the early 1960s, the Soviet Union was developing many classes of tactical and strategic nuclear weapons, making it less vulnerable to a US nuclear attack. In such circumstances, MC14/2 became far less acceptable to western military planners, who consequently sought to develop a more flexible nuclear posture for Nato. This became known as 'flexible response'. It involved the ability to respond to Soviet military actions with a wide range of military forces, but also with the provision that nuclear weapons could be used first in such a way as to force the Soviet Union to halt any aggression and withdraw. Once again, it embodied the belief that a nuclear war could be fought and won.

The new flexible-response doctrine was progressively accepted by Nato member-states in 1967 and 1968. It was codified in a document entitled *Overall Strategic Concept for the Defence of the NATO Area*, or MC14/3. It was a posture with one particular advantage for the United States: that it might avoid nuclear weapons being used against its own territory.

A US army colonel expressed this rather candidly at the time, writing that the strategy:

> 'recognizes the need for a capability to cope with situations short of general nuclear war and undertakes to maintain a forward posture designed to keep such situations as far away from the United States as possible' (see Walter Beinke, 'Flexible Response in Perspective', *Military Review*, November 1968).

Flexible response was to remain in operation for most of the last quarter century of the Cold War, including periods of considerable tension in the early 1980s. Operational plans for nuclear use were (and are) developed by the nuclear activities branch of the Supreme Headquarters Allied Powers Europe (Shape) near Mons in Belgium, operating in conjunction with the US joint strategic target planning staff responsible for the Single Integrated Operational Plan (Siop) strategic nuclear posture from its base in Omaha, Nebraska.

By the early 1970s, flexible response was well established under Nato's nuclear operations plan which embraced two levels of the use of tactical nuclear weapons against Soviet forces: selective options and general response. Selective options involved a variety of plans, many of them assuming first use of nuclear weapons against Warsaw Pact conventional forces. At the smallest level, these could include up to five small air-burst nuclear detonations intended as warning shots to demonstrate Nato's intent.

At a rather higher level of use were the so-called pre-packaged options involving up to 100 nuclear weapons. The US army field manual at the time defined such a package as:

> 'a group of nuclear weapons of specific yields for use in a specific area and within a limited time to support a specific tactical goal ... Each package must contain nuclear weapons sufficient to alter the tactical situation decisively and to accomplish the mission' (see *Operations: FM 100-5*, US Department of the Army, 1982).

While these different levels of selective use were thought to be possible ways of winning a nuclear war, the possibility remained that this would fail, and a more general nuclear exchange would result. This was the second level of use of tactical nuclear weapons; it was termed a general nuclear response in which Nato nuclear forces in Europe would be used on a massive scale along with US strategic forces.

Thus, by the end of the 1970s, Nato had developed a flexible-response strategy that involved detailed planning for the selective first use of nuclear weapons in the belief that a limited nuclear war could be won. By the early 1980s, with highly accurate fast ballistic missiles such as the Pershing 2 being deployed by the United States, there were indications that Nato was even moving to a policy of early first use of nuclear weapons.

One indication of this came in a remarkably candid interview given by the Nato supreme commander, General Bernard W Rogers. He said that his orders were:

> 'Before you lose the cohesiveness of the alliance – that is, before you are subject to (conventional Soviet military) penetration on a fairly broad scale – you *will* request, not you may, but you *will* request the use of nuclear weapons ... [emphasis in the original].'
> (*International Defense Review*, February 1986).

The long-standing Nato policy of the first use of nuclear weapons was not promoted widely in public, where all the emphasis was placed on nuclear weapons as an ultimate deterrent. Even so, the policy was made clear on relatively rare occasions. One example is evidence from the UK's Ministry of Defence to a Parliamentary select committee in 1988:

> 'The fundamental objective of maintaining the capability for selective sub-strategic use of theatre weapons is political – to demonstrate in advance that NATO has the capability and will to use nuclear weapons in a deliberate, politically-controlled way with the objective of restoring deterrence by inducing the aggressor to terminate his aggression and withdraw.'

With the ending of the Cold War and the collapse of the Soviet Union in 1989-91, there was some easing of Nato nuclear policy. This included the withdrawal of a substantial proportion of Nato nuclear weapons from western Europe as the Soviet Union withdrew from its former satellites in east-central Europe. The possibility of first use was considered increasingly unlikely, but not abandoned as a facet of Nato policy.

Although the Soviet Union is no more, Nato nuclear planning still involves a policy of first use, British nuclear weapons remain committed to Nato, and the United States still maintains tactical nuclear bombs at one of its remaining bases in the UK, Lakenheath in Suffolk, in eastern England.

Britain's independent targeting

Since the 1950s, Britain has deployed nuclear weapons on many occasions outside the immediate Nato area of western and southern Europe and the north Atlantic. This included the basing of RAF nuclear-capable strike aircraft in Cyprus in the 1960s and 1970s, regular detachments of V-bombers to RAF Tengah in Singapore in the mid-1960s, and the deployment of Scimitar and Buccaneer nuclear-capable strike aircraft on the Royal Navy's aircraft carriers from 1962 to 1978. Nuclear weapons were also carried on four task-force ships during the Falklands/Malvinas War of 1982.

This long history of 'out-of-area' deployments of nuclear weapons by Britain is matched by a number of indications of a willingness to use them in limited conflicts. In one of the few published studies of British tactical nuclear targeting, Milan Rai wrote in his 1994 paper *Tactical Trident* (Drava Papers):

> 'Sir John Slessor, Marshall of the RAF in the 1950s, and one of the most influential military theorists of the period, believed that "In most of the possible theatres of limited war ... it must be accepted that it is at least improbable that we would be able to meet a major communist offensive in one of these areas without resorting to tactical nuclear weapons".'

This statement was made by a senior military figure rather than a politician, but similar comments did come from more official government sources. In 1955, the then Defence Minister (and later Prime Minister) Harold Macmillan stated in the House of Commons:

> '... the power of interdiction upon invading columns by nuclear weapons gives a new aspect altogether to strategy, both in the Middle East and the Far East. It affords a breathing space, an interval, a short but perhaps vital opportunity for the assembly, during the battle for air supremacy, of larger conventional forces than can normally be stationed in those areas.'

Such an idea of a small nuclear war was further expressed during the 1957 defence debate by Macmillan's successor as defence minister, Duncan Sandys:

> 'one must distinguish between major global war, involving a head on clash between the great Powers, and minor conflicts which can be localised and which do not bring the great Powers into direct collision. Limited and localised acts of aggression, for example, by a satellite Communist State could, no doubt, be resisted with conventional arms, or, at worst, with tactical nuclear weapons, the use of which could be confined to the battle area.'

A tranche of British government letters, held in the national archives and released on 29 June 2006, provides further documentary evidence of this willingness to use nuclear weapons in the very period Macmillan and Sandys were speaking. One letter from Defence Minister Harold Wilkinson in 1961 refers to a possible Chinese attack on Hong Kong (then a British colony), and says: 'Our object is to encourage the Chinese to believe than an attack on Hong Kong would involve US nuclear retaliation.'

This historical context raises the question as to whether the smaller sub-strategic Trident warheads, or indeed the more powerful strategic versions, might be used independently of Nato. Britain reserves this right, and one of the more detailed assessments of the range of options for sub-strategic Trident warheads was made in the authoritative military journal *International Defence Review* in 1994:

> 'At what might be called the "upper end" of the usage spectrum, they could be used in a conflict involving large-scale forces (including British ground and air forces), such as the 1990-91 Gulf War, to reply to an enemy nuclear strike. Secondly, they could be used in a similar setting, but to reply to enemy use of weapons of mass destruction, such as bacteriological or chemical weapons, for which the British possess no like-for-like retaliatory capability. Thirdly, they could be used in a demonstrative role: i.e. aimed at a non-critical uninhabited area, with the message that if the country concerned continued on its present course of action, nuclear weapons would be aimed at a high-priority target. Finally, there is the punitive role, where a country has committed an act, despite specific warnings that to do so would incur a nuclear strike (see David Miller, 'Britain Ponders Single Warhead Option', *International Defence Review*, September 1994).

It is worth noting that three of the four circumstances envisaged involve the first use of nuclear weapons by Britain.

Such issues rarely surface in the public arena, but concern has been expressed in Parliament that the government has not been sufficiently clear about the circumstances under which British nuclear weapons would be used in post-Cold War circumstances. For example, the House of Commons Defence Select Committee noted in 1998:

> 'We regret that there has been no restatement of nuclear policy since the speech of the then Secretary of State in 1993; the SDR [Strategic Defence Review] does not provide a new statement of the government's nuclear deterrent posture in the present strategic situation within which the sub-strategic role of Trident could be clarified. We recommend the clarification of both the UK's strategic and sub-strategic policy.'

This was, in part, in response to comments made to the committee by the then Secretary of State for Defence, George (now Lord) Robertson. He had told the Committee that the sub-strategic option was 'an option available that is other than guaranteed to lead to a full scale nuclear exchange'. He envisaged that a nuclear-armed country might wish to '... use a sub-strategic weapon, making it clear that it is sub-strategic in order to show that ... if the attack continues [the country] would then go to the full strategic strike,' and that this would give a chance to 'stop the escalation on the lower point of the ladder'.

This statement indicated that 'a country', such as Britain, could consider using nuclear weapons without initiating an all-out nuclear war, and that the government therefore appeared to accept the view that a limited nuclear war could be fought and won. It was evidently not the clear statement that the Committee sought, and it did not indicate the circumstances in which such weapons might be used. In particular, it did not appear to relate to whether Britain or British forces had already been attacked with nuclear weapons, or whether nuclear weapons would be used first in response to other circumstances.

The Iraq wars

At the same time, there had been no evidence to suggest that Britain had moved away from the nuclear posture of the Cold War era that included the possibility of using nuclear weapons first. Indeed, just as the Cold War was winding down, the first Iraq war in early 1991 was one occasion when British nuclear use might have been considered. As the UK forces embarked for the Gulf in September 1990, *The Observer* reported that Britain was prepared to retaliate to an Iraqi chemical attack with nuclear weapons:

> 'A senior officer attached to Britain's 7th Armoured Brigade, which began to leave for the Gulf yesterday, claims that if UK forces are attacked with chemical gas by Iraqi troops, they will retaliate with battlefield nuclear weapons. The Ministry of Defence refused to confirm this last night, but it is the first unofficial indication that British troops might be authorised to use nuclear weapons to defend themselves if attacked' (see *Observer*, 30 September 1990, front page).

More than a decade later and prior to the start of the second Iraq war in 2003, the then Secretary of State for Defence, Geoff Hoon, was questioned by members of the select committee and appeared to indicate that Britain maintained this policy. In relation to a state such as Iraq he said: 'They can be absolutely confident that in the right conditions we would be willing to use our nuclear weapons.'

This exchange did not make clear whether this would be in response to a nuclear attack initiated by a state such as Iraq. Hoon was questioned on this point on 24 March 2002 on the Jonathan Dimbleby programme on ITV. He was asked whether nuclear use might be in response to non-nuclear weapons such as chemical or biological weapons. He replied:

> 'Let me make it clear the long-standing British government policy that if our forces or our people were threatened by weapons of mass destruction we would reserve the right to use appropriate proportionate responses which might ... might in extreme circumstances include the use of nuclear weapons.'

Later in the exchange, Hoon made it clear that he could envisage circumstances in which British nuclear weapons were used in response to chemical or biological weapons. He was later asked by Dimbleby: 'But you would only use Britain's weapon of mass destruction after an attack by Saddam Hussein using weapons of mass destruction?'

Hoon replied: 'Clearly if there were strong evidence of an imminent attack if we knew that an attack was about to occur and we could use our weapons to protect against it.'

The implication of this is clear – that there are circumstances where Britain would consider using nuclear weapons in response to a non-nuclear attack involving chemical or biological weapons and would even consider using nuclear weapons to pre-empt such an attack.

A time for air

Britain has deployed nuclear forces for almost fifty years. For most of that time, they have been primarily committed to Nato, which has maintained a nuclear-targeting posture that includes the first use of nuclear weapons. Britain also retains the capability to use nuclear weapons independently.

Although the publicly acknowledged 'declaratory' policy remains one of 'last resort' use of nuclear weapons, the 'deployment' policy involves the idea of nuclear war-fighting that falls far short of responding to a nuclear attack on Britain. This is the long-standing reality. It could certainly liven up the forthcoming debate on replacing Trident if this enduring feature of British nuclear-weapons policy got a really thorough airing.

This article by Paul Rogers was originally published on openDemocracy.net under a Creative Commons Licence.

Common Sense and Nuclear Warfare
by Bertrand Russell

Available for the first time in many years, *Common Sense and Nuclear Warfare* presents Russell's keen insights into the threat of nuclear conflict, and his argument that the only way to end this threat is to end war itself.

Written at the height of the Cold War, this volume is crucial for understanding Russell's involvement in the Campaign for Nuclear Disarmament and his passionate campaigning for peace.

It remains an extremely important book in today's uncertain nuclear world, and is essential reading for all those interested in Russell and postwar history.

Includes a new introduction by Ken Coates, Chairman of The Bertrand Russell Peace Foundation

Paperback Price: £11.99 | ISBN: 9780415249959
Hardback Price: £55.00 | ISBN: 9780415259942

www.routledge.com   Available from all good bookshops

Nuclear dependency

John Ainslie

John Ainslie is coordinator of the Scottish Campaign for Nuclear Disarmament. These excerpts are from The Future of the British Bomb, *his comprehensive review of the issues raised by nuclear-armed Trident missiles carried on four British submarines, and their possible replacement, or not. He begins by examining Britain's dependence on the United States for parts for Trident's warheads. Published by the WMD Awareness Programme, the full report is available online (www.banthebomb.org/future. doc).*

The British Government acknowledges that Trident missiles are leased from the United States but claims that they carry British warheads. This description is questionable. The warhead is a copy of the US W76. A report by the Public Records Office refers to the Anglicisation of an American design. Several key components are produced in America. The warheads on Royal Navy Trident submarines could be more accurately described as Anglo-American rather than British.

The Neutron Generator is one vital part. It contributes to the initiation of nuclear fission. The MC2989 Neutron Generators initially deployed on British warheads were overhauled in the US in 1999. This implies that they were built there. A replacement Neutron Generator, MC4380, was manufactured in America and supplied to Britain in 2002. The Gas Reservoir in the warhead supplies tritium to boost the fission process. The reservoirs on British warheads are filled with tritium in the US. These are difficult components to build. This suggests that the reservoirs in British warheads are manufactured in America. The Arming, Fusing and Firing System triggers the warhead. The model used on British warheads was designed by Sandia Laboratory and almost certainly procured off-the-shelf from America.

The Trident system operated by Britain is not identical to that deployed by the US Navy, although it is very similar. One difference is the type of high explosive in the British warhead. US nuclear weapons laboratories are playing a critical role in assessing the long-term performance of this British explosive. A second difference is the Fire Control System. British submarines carry a slightly different model. But all the hardware and software for it is created in America. It is significant that, even where the British Trident system differs from the American version, US support is essential.

The US role in handling tritium and making the Neutron Generators is known from publicly available American sources. Yet when asked about these issues in Parliament the Defence Minister refused to answer, on grounds of national security. Successive governments have withheld information to conceal dependence. There is a deliberate attempt to create ambiguity over the extent of dependence. The true limitations of independence are concealed. This is consistent with the policy of uncertainty that lies at the heart of British nuclear policy.

Reliance on American support is not only of historical and current significance. It will remain a crucial factor so long as Britain remains a nuclear-weapons state. The terms of the Mutual Defence Agreement [between the United Kingdom and the United States] constrain how information and material that has been exchanged can be used. The British nuclear weapons establishment today is almost entirely dependent on this information. Any future nuclear programme will build on what exists today. It will be subject to the same limitations and must be in the mutual defence interest of both Britain and the United States.

A truly independent nuclear weapons programme is not an option. A future system might be more or less dependent on US support than at present. Current and future US Administrations will determine the degree of independence. Also, the US can probably restrict the independence of the system in service, should there be a change in policy in Washington.

Targeting systems

In 1988, the National Audit Office reported that it was essential that Trident targeting software be produced in Britain. As Trident entered service it was revealed that 'contractor support' had been required to complete this work. This contractor support almost certainly came from the United States.

Targeting data on British Trident submarines is processed in the Fire Control System by software produced in America. This data is created in the Nuclear Operations and Targeting Centre in London. The centre relies on US software. In 2002 the Fire Control Systems on British and American Trident submarines were modified. Just before this the computers in the London targeting centre were upgraded. The American applications used for target planning and for fire control are complex and unique. It would be possible for US programmers to modify the software supplied to Britain, either openly or covertly, to restrict how Trident could be used. Even those who operate the system may not have an accurate perception of its dependence. The British Trident system is only as independent as Washington wants it to be. It could be argued that constraints on independence would be consistent with the Mutual Defence Agreement.

British warheads can be integrated into US attack plans. There are special arrangements for supplying US nuclear targeting information to Britain. The United Kingdom Liaison Cell at STRATCOM [Strategic Command] headquarters in Omaha plays a central role in this process. US support may also be required to produce plans for an independent attack.

The Nato Nuclear Planning System is a mechanism for preparing attacks by nuclear-armed aircraft. The crucial systems for targeting Britain's Trident force are bilateral. While there will be links between the British system and Nato headquarters, the essential networking is between London and the headquarters of STRATCOM. The instructions to order the use of British weapons are not issued in the form of Nato Emergency Action Messages, but through a unique system.

Trident missiles can only achieve the required level of accuracy if a special forecast of the weather over the target is available. This is supplied to British and American submarines in compressed messages transmitted every 12 hours by the US Navy. Trident also relies on gravity information from US sources. Without this weather and gravity data the missiles would be less accurate.

British Trident submarines are normally on a state of alert measured in days. There is a substantial American presence at the Northwood headquarters from where British submarine operations are controlled. If the alert state of British Trident were raised, the US would almost certainly know. This would give them several days' notice of any British nuclear attack.

Communications with British Trident submarines can be made through British or Nato systems. In addition there are bilateral systems. These are likely to be used for key data. Submarines can receive messages on a wide range of frequencies. In future it will be possible to use Extremely High Frequency (EHF), but only through a transmitter on an American satellite. EHF is important because it is considered to be less vulnerable than other systems during a nuclear war.

* * *

The effects of nuclear use

A single Trident warhead used against a military installation, such as a naval base in Northern Russia, could cause around 23,000 civilian fatalities. If the target was inside a city then there could be 150,000 – 200,000 deaths. If the warheads from one British submarine were exploded at military targets in the Moscow area, most of them outside the city, this could result in around 3 million deaths. This figure would rise to between 9 and 30 million if the warheads on all three armed submarines were detonated. These figures only include short-term fatalities. The long-term effects of radiation, environmental damage and the destruction of infrastructure would substantially increase the death rate. Studies have shown that a US counterforce attack on strategic military targets in Russia would result in massive civilian casualties. The raw figures do not give a true picture of the horror that would be inflicted on individual women, men and children. The photographs and accounts from Hiroshima and Nagasaki provide a glimpse of the monstrosity of nuclear weapons.

Accident

A US study distinguishes three types of nuclear accident scenario. The first situation is an unauthorised launch of a weapon by a rogue commander or a terrorist. The second is where a launch takes places by mistake, as a result of a training accident or a system malfunction. The third scenario is where incorrect information results in an intentional launch.

A number of situations fall into this third category. There could be an error or malfunction in the early-warning systems which are designed to detect a missile attack. A non-threatening event could be misinterpreted. There could be a false perception that another country had launched a nuclear attack, or a misperception that a nuclear weapon had detonated within the homeland. Lastly, a training attack could be misinterpreted as a real attack.

The report touches on the connections between the possession of nuclear weapons, relations between Russia and the US, and the risk of accidental use. It suggests that de-alerting moves could improve relations between the two countries and so provide a basis for more substantial measures. It recommends that several immediate unilateral measures be taken within 6 to 12 months. One proposal is to move Trident submarines further from Russia. Britain's Trident force is not mentioned, but for geographical reasons it could be seen as a particular threat because of the proximity of patrol areas to Russia.

The analysis concludes, 'The risk of accidental or unauthorised nuclear use is too high given the markedly improved relationship between the United States and Russia. This is in part because nuclear weapons now play a role out of proportion to other aspects of the relationship'. Adherence to nuclear deterrence is an obstacle to progress towards lowering risks and improving relations – 'A central reason for the phased approach is that some options for improving safety would push too far beyond current deterrence practices and orthodoxies to be acceptable'.

The risk of a nuclear weapons accident has been considered particularly in the context of the large American and Russian arsenals on a high state of alert. But the dangers also apply to other nuclear powers. For Britain's part there is a need to recognise that our nuclear weapons contribute to the risk of an accident. Also each step that we take towards disarmament will contribute to building a better relationship with Russia. What is blocking progress is continued adherence to outdated and dangerous theories about nuclear deterrence.

Financial costs

Cost will be a major factor determining the future of British nuclear weapons. Michael Quinlan [civil servant] concedes that if today he had to decide whether or not to embark on the Trident programme then the cost would not be justified. Admiral Sir Raymond Lygo suggested that the cost of Trident should be capped at a level relative to the threat from Russia and China.

A complete rebuild of a Trident-like system would cost over £15 billion. If the submarines are replaced, each one would come with a price tag of more than £1 billion. A substantial warhead upgrade would be very expensive and building a new weapon would cost more again. A significant proportion of any new expenditure would go to American contractors.

The official estimate of the annual cost of the nuclear weapons programme is between 2 and 3 per cent of the defence budget. This is equivalent to between £700 million and £1 billion each year. Taken over the 30-year life of a system this adds up to between £21 billion and £30 billion, more than the capital cost.

The substantial overheads of the nuclear-powered submarine programme are partly due to Trident and partly to the conventionally-armed force. The primary mission of the latter is the protection of Trident. There are huge potential savings to be made by giving up nuclear-powered submarines. Estimates of the cost of decommissioning defence nuclear facilities have increased several times in recent years. The long-term costs of storing nuclear waste will increase with each year Britain continues to have nuclear weapons and nuclear-powered submarines.

In assessing the cost of upgrading Trident, or acquiring a replacement, the budget should include not only capital costs but also the total revenue cost throughout the planned life of the system, including decommissioning.

References available on request

COMMUNICATION WORKERS UNION

Campaigning Against Nuclear Replacement to Trident

Billy Hayes
General Secretary

Andy Kerr
President

Fates worse than DEATH

Kurt Vonnegut

Kurt Vonnegut sent us this article in 1982, as a contribution to the discussion surrounding the first European Conference for European Nuclear Disarmament in Brussels. The foreword, by Ken Coates, describes the background to that event. We reprint it 24 years after its first appearance, because, unfortunately, it still maintains all its relevance.

Foreword

A little over two years ago, the Russell Foundation launched an Appeal for European Nuclear Disarmament. We were scared. The arms race was running wild, and the big nuclear powers were threatening each other as if the next war were going to be fought with catapults. Thousands of people agreed with our Appeal, and signed it. Among them was Kurt Vonnegut Jnr, who knows about war at first hand because he was a prisoner of war in Dresden when allied bombers burnt that city, and almost everyone in it.

For two years now, we have been trying to organise a European Conference of all the disarmament movements. At last this is scheduled to meet in Brussels, on 2nd, 3rd and 4th July 1982. After that, we hope to move on to a second big conference in Berlin during 1983.

I think these meetings will succeed. They have to succeed, because the peace movements absolutely have to speak to one another, exchange ideas, learn to share each other's experiences, problems and successes.

But in one way, however many people come to Brussels, the END Convention is already a great success. And that is because of Kurt Vonnegut. I wrote to him to ask him for a message to the Convention. In fact, I wrote more than once, but in the end he replied. This is what he said:

2 June 1982
Dear Ken Coates,
I'm sorry to have been such a slovenly responder to your good letters. I can't come to Brussels in July, but the world seems to be one big city now. I ran into the Mayor of Nagasaki, whose mother was pregnant with him when the bomb was dropped, only this afternoon – two hundred yards from my doorstep. As it turns out, he is for peace. Surprise.

I, a druid, preached for peace at the Episcopal Cathedral here, St. John the Divine, two Sundays ago. I enclose a copy of what I said, more or less. If anything in it is of any use to you, please help yourself. The copyright is owned by the Cathedral, which paid me zero. They wouldn't have the balls to sue, no matter what you did.

Cheers,

Kurt Vonnegut

The piece he sent is a gem. Opening that letter was nicer than being given a parcel of diamonds as big as marbles. In the middle of the Falkland war, with people dying and threatened with death, this is the finest message we could have had for the delegates to the Brussels meeting.

Ken Coates

* * *

Fates worse than Death

Kurt Vonnegut
Lecture at St. John the Divine, NYC 23 May 1982

Good morning,
This is a pretty small church, but I guess I have to start somewhere.

Actually, this is not my main line of work. Preaching in Cathedrals is just a hobby. I make up stories for a living. I get my ideas from dreams.

The wildest dream I have had so far is about *The New Yorker Magazine*. In this dream, the magazine has published a three-part essay by Jonathan Schell, which proves that life on Earth is about to end. I am supposed to go to the largest Gothic cathedral in the world, where all the people are waiting, and say something wonderful – right before a hydrogen bomb is dropped on the Empire State Building.

People as far away as Bridgeport will die instantly.

Here is how I interpret the dream: I consider myself an important writer, and I think *The New Yorker* should be ashamed that it has never published me.

* * *

I will speak today about the worst imaginable consequences of doing without hydrogen bombs. This should be a relief. I am sure you are sick and tired of hearing how all living things sizzle and pop inside a radioactive fireball. We have known that for more than a third of this century – ever since we dropped an atom bomb on the yellow people of Hiroshima. They certainly sizzled and popped.

After all is said and done, what was that sizzling and popping, despite the brilliant technology which caused it, but our old friend death? Let us not forget that Saint Joan of Arc was made to sizzle and pop in old times with nothing more than firewood. She wound up dead. The people of Hiroshima wound up dead. Dead is dead.

Scientists, for all their creativity, will never discover a method for making people deader than dead. So if some of you are worried about being hydrogen-bombed, you are merely fearing death. There is nothing new in that. If there weren't any hydrogen bombs, death would still be after you. And what is death but an absence of life? That's all it is. That is all it ever can be.

Death is nothing. What is all this fuss about?

* * *

Let us 'up the ante', as gamblers say. Let us talk about fates worse than death. When the Reverend Jim Jones saw that his followers in Guyana were facing fates worse than death, he gave them Kool-Aid laced with cyanide. If our government sees that we are facing fates worse than death, it will shower our enemies with hydrogen bombs, and then we will be showered in turn. There will be plenty of Kool-Aid for everyone, in a manner of speaking, when the right time comes.

What will the right time look like?

I will not waste your time with trivial fates, which are only marginally worse than death. Suppose we were conquered by an enemy, for example, who didn't understand our wonderful economic system, and so Braniff Airlines and International Harvester and so on all went bust, and millions of Americans who wanted to work couldn't find any jobs anywhere. Or suppose we were conquered by an enemy who was too cheap to take good care of children and old people. Or suppose we were conquered by an enemy who wouldn't spend money on anything but weapons for World War Three. These are all tribulations we could live with, if we had to – although God forbid.

But suppose we foolishly got rid of our nuclear weapons, our Kool-Aid, and an enemy came over here and crucified us. Crucifixion was the most painful thing which the ancient Romans ever found to do to anyone. They knew as much about pain as we do about genocide. They sometimes crucified hundreds of people at one time. That is what they did to all the survivors of the army of Spartacus, which was composed mostly of escaped slaves. They crucified them all. There were several miles of crosses.

If we were up on crosses, with nails through our feet and hands, wouldn't we wish that we still had hydrogen bombs, so that life could be ended everywhere? Absolutely.

We know of one person who was crucified in olden times, who was supposedly as capable as we or the Russians are of ending life everywhere. But he chose to endure agony instead. All he said was, 'Forgive them, Father – they know not what they do.'

He let life go on, as awful as it was for him, because here we are, aren't we?

But he was a special case. It is unfair to use Jesus Christ as an exemplar of how much pain and humiliation we ordinary human beings should put up with before calling for the end of everything.

* * *

I don't believe that we are about to be crucified. No potential enemy we now face has anywhere near enough carpenters. Not even the Pentagon at budget time has mentioned crucifixion. I am sorry to have to put that idea into their heads. I will have only myself to blame if, a year from now, the Joint Chiefs of Staff testify under oath that we are on the brink of being crucified.

But what if they said, instead, that we would be enslaved if we did not appropriate enough money for weaponry? That could be true. Despite our worldwide reputation for sloppy workmanship, wouldn't some enemy get a kick out of forcing us into involuntary servitude, buying and selling us like so many household appliances or farm machines or inflatable erotic toys?

And slavery would surely be a fate worse than death. We can agree on that, I'm sure. We should send a message to the Pentagon: 'If Americans are about to become enslaved, it is Kool-Aid Time.'

They will know what we mean.

* * *

Of course, at Kool-Aid time all higher forms of life on Earth, not just us and our enemies, will be killed. Even those beautiful and fearless and utterly stupid sea birds, the blue-footed boobies of the Galapagos Islands, will die, because we object to slavery.

I have seen those birds, by the way – up close. I could have unscrewed their heads, if I wanted to. I made a trip to the Galapagos Islands two months ago – in the company of, among other people, Paul Moore, the bishop of this very cathedral.

That is the sort of company I keep these days – everything from bishops to blue-footed boobies. I have never seen a human slave, though. But my four great-grandfathers saw slaves. When they came to this country in search of justice and opportunity, there were millions of Americans who were slaves.

* * *

The equation which links a strong defence posture to not being enslaved is laid down in that stirring fight song, much heard lately, 'Rule Britannia'. I will sing the equation:

'Rule, Britannia, Britannia rule the waves –'

That, of course, is a poetic demand for a navy second to none. The next line explains why it is essential to have a navy that good:

'Britons never, never, never shall be slaves.'

It may surprise some of you to learn what an old equation that is. The Scottish poet who wrote it, James Thomson, died in 1748 – one quarter of a century before there was such a country as the United States of America. Thomson promised Britons that they would never be slaves at a time when the enslavement of persons with inferior weaponry was a respectable industry. Plenty of people were going to be slaves, and it would serve them right, too – but Britons would not be among them.

So that isn't really a very nice song. It is about not being humiliated which is all right. But it is also about humiliating others, which is not a moral thing to do. The humiliation of others should never be a national goal.

There is one poet who should have been ashamed of himself.

* * *

If the Soviet Union came over here and enslaved us, it wouldn't be the first time Americans were slaves. If we conquered the Russians and enslaved them, it wouldn't be the first time Russians were slaves.

And the last time Americans were slaves, and the last time Russians were slaves, they displayed astonishing spiritual strengths and resourcefulness. They were good at loving one another. They trusted God. They discovered in the simplest, most natural satisfactions, reasons to be glad to be alive. They were able to believe that better days were coming in the sweet by-and-by. And here is a fascinating statistic: they committed suicide less often than their masters did.

So Americans and Russians can both stand slavery, if they have to – and still want life to go on and on.

Could it be that slavery isn't a fate worse than death. After all, people are tough, you know? Maybe we shouldn't send that message to the Pentagon – about slavery and Kool-Aid time.

* * *

But suppose enemies came ashore in great numbers, because we lacked the means to stop them, and they pushed us out of our homes and off our ancestral lands, and into swamps and deserts. Suppose that they even tried to destroy our religion, telling us that our Great God Jehovah, or whatever we wanted to call Him, was as ridiculous as a piece of junk jewellery.

Again: this is a wringer millions of Americans have already been through – or are still going through. It is another catastrophe which Americans can endure, if they have to – and still, miraculously, maintain some measure of dignity, or self-respect.

As bad as life is for our Indians, they still like it better than death.

* * *

So I haven't had much luck, have I, in identifying fates worse than death. Crucifixion is the only clear winner so far, and we aren't about to be crucified. We aren't about to be enslaved, either – to be treated as white Americans used to treat black Americans. And no potential enemy that I have heard of wants to come over here to treat all of us the way we still treat American Indians.

What other fates worse than death could I name? Life without petroleum?

* * *

In melodramas of a century ago, a female's loss of virginity outside of holy wedlock was sometimes spoken as a fate worse than death. I hope that isn't what the Pentagon or the Kremlin has in mind – but you never know.

I would rather die for virginity than for petroleum, I think. It's more literary, somehow.

* * *

I may be blinding myself to the racist aspects of hydrogen bombs, whose only function is to end everything. Perhaps there are tribulations which white people should not be asked to tolerate. But the Russian slaves were white. The supposedly unenslavable Britons were enslaved by the Romans. Even proud Britons, if they were enslaved now, would have to say, 'Here we go again'. Armenians and Jews have certainly been treated hideously in modern as well as ancient times – and they have still wanted life to go on and on and on. About a third of our own white people were robbed and ruined and scorned after our Civil War. They still wanted life to go on and on and on.

* * *

Have there ever been large numbers of human beings of any sort who have not, despite everything, done everything they could to keep life going on and on and on?
Soldiers.
'Death before Dishonour' was the motto of several military formations during the Civil War – on both sides. It may be the motto of the Eighty-second Airborne Division right now. A motto like that made a certain amount of sense, I suppose, when military death was what happened to the soldier on the right or the left of you – or in front of you – or in back of you. But military death now can easily mean the death of everything, including, as I have already said, the blue-footed boobies of the Galapagos Islands.
The webbed feet of those birds really are the brightest blue, by the way. When two blue-footed boobies begin a courtship, they show each other what beautiful, bright blue feet they have.

* * *

If you go to the Galapagos Islands, and see all the strange creatures, you are bound to think what Charles Darwin thought when he went there: How much time Nature has in which to accomplish simply anything. If we desolate this planet, Nature can get life going again. All it takes is a few million years or so, the wink of an eye to Nature.
Only humankind is running out of time.
My guess is that we will not disarm, even though we should, and that we really will blow up everything by and by. History shows that human beings are vicious enough to commit every imaginable atrocity, including the construction of factories whose only purpose was to kill people and burn them up.
It may be that we were put here on Earth to blow the place to smithereens. We may be Nature's way of creating new galaxies. We may be programmed to improve and improve our weapons, and to believe that death is better than dishonour.

And then, one day, as disarmament rallies are being held all over the planet, ka-blooey! A new Milky Way is born.

* * *

Perhaps we should be adoring instead of loathing our hydrogen bombs. They could be the eggs for new galaxies.

* * *

What can save us? Divine intervention, certainly – and this is the place to ask for it. We might pray to be rescued from our inventiveness, just as the dinosaurs may have prayed to be rescued from their size.

But the inventiveness which we so regret now may also be giving us, along with the rockets and warheads, the means to achieve what has hitherto been an impossibility, the unity of mankind. I am talking mainly about television sets.

Even in my own lifetime, it used to be necessary for a young soldier to get into fighting before he became disillusioned about war. His parents back home were equally ignorant, and believed him to be slaying monsters. But now, thanks to modern communications, the people of every industrialised nation are nauseated by war by the time they are ten years old. America's first generation of television viewers has gone to war and come home again – and we have never seen veterans like them before.

What makes the Vietnam veterans so somehow spooky? We could almost describe them as being 'unwholesomely mature'. They have never had illusions about war. They are the first soldiers in history who knew even in childhood, from having heard and seen so many pictures of actual and restaged battles, that war is meaningless butchery of ordinary people like themselves.

It used to be that veterans could shock their parents when they came home, as Ernest Hemingway did, by announcing that everything about war was repulsive and stupid and dehumanising. But the parents of our Vietnam veterans were disillusioned about war, too, many of them having seen it first hand, before their children ever went overseas. Thanks to modern communications, Americans of all ages were dead sick of war even before we went into Vietnam.

Thanks to modern communications, the poor, unlucky young people from the Soviet Union, now killing and dying in Afghanistan, were dead sick of war before they ever got there.

Thanks to modern communications, the same must be true of the poor, unlucky young people from Argentina and Great Britain, now killing and dying in the Falkland Islands. *The New York Post* calls them 'Argies' and 'Brits'. Thanks to modern communications, we know that they are a good deal more marvellous and complicated than that, and that what is happening to them down there, on the rim of the Antarctic, is a lot more horrible and shameful than a soccer match.

* * *

When I was a boy it was unusual for an American, or a person of any nationality, for that matter, to know much about foreigners. Those who did were specialists – diplomats, explorers, journalists, anthropologists. And they usually knew a lot about just a few groups of foreigners, Eskimos, maybe, or Arabs, or what have you. To them, as to the schoolchildren of Indianapolis, large areas of the globe were *terra incognita*.

Now look what has happened. Thanks to modern communications, we have seen sights and heard sounds from virtually every square mile of the land mass on this planet. Millions of us have actually visited more exotic places than had many explorers during my childhood. Many of you have been to Timbuktu. Many of you have been to Katmandu. My dentist just got home from Fiji. He told me all about Fiji. If he had taken his fingers out of my mouth, I would have told him about the Galapagos Islands.

So we now know for certain that there are no potential human enemies anywhere who are anything but human beings almost exactly like ourselves. They need food. How amazing. They love their children. How amazing. They obey their leaders. How amazing. They think like their neighbours. How amazing.

Thanks to modern communications, we now have something we never had before: reason to mourn deeply the death or wounding of any human being on any side in any war.

* * *

It was because of rotten communications, of malicious, racist ignorance that we were able to celebrate the killing of almost all the inhabitants in Hiroshima, Japan, thirty-seven years ago. We thought they were vermin. They thought we were vermin. They would have clapped their little yellow hands with glee, and grinned with their crooked buck teeth, if they could have incinerated everybody in Kansas City, say.

Thanks to how much the people of the world now know about all the other people of the world, the fun of killing enemies has lost its zing. It has so lost its zing that no sane citizen of the Soviet Union, if we were to go to war with that society, would feel anything but horror if his country were to kill practically everybody in New York and Chicago and San Francisco. Killing enemies has so lost its zing that no sane citizen of the United States would feel anything but horror if our country were to kill practically everybody in Moscow and Leningrad and Kiev.

Or in Nagasaki, Japan, for that matter.

We have often heard it said that people would have to change, or we would go on having world wars. I bring you good news this morning: people have changed.

We aren't so ignorant and bloodthirsty any more.

* * *

I told you a crazy dream I had – about *The New Yorker Magazine* and this cathedral. I will tell you a sane dream now.

I dreamed last night of our descendants a thousand years from now, which is to say all of humanity. If you are at all into reproduction, as was the Emperor Charlemagne, you can pick up an awful lot of relatives in a thousand years. Every person in this cathedral who has a drop of white blood, is a descendant of Charlemagne.

A thousand years from now, if there are still human beings on Earth, every one of those human beings will be descended from us – and from everyone who has chosen to reproduce.

In my dream, our descendants are numerous. Some of them are rich, some are poor, some are likeable, some are insufferable.

I ask them how humanity, against all odds, managed to keep going for another millennium. They tell me that they and their ancestors did it by preferring life over death for themselves and others at every opportunity, even at the expense of being dishonoured. They endured all sorts of insults and humiliations and disappointments without committing either suicide or murder. They are also the people who do the insulting and humiliating and disappointing.

I endear myself to them by suggesting a motto they might like to put on their belt buckles or tee-shirts or whatever. They aren't all hippies, by the way. They aren't all Americans, either. They aren't even all white people.

I give them a quotation from that great 19th century moralist and robber baron, Jim Fisk, who may have contributed money to this cathedral.

Jim Fisk uttered his famous words after a particularly disgraceful episode having to do with the Erie Railroad. Fisk himself had no choice but to find himself contemptible. He thought this over, and then he shrugged and said what we all must learn to say, if we want to go on living much longer:

'Nothing is lost save honour.'

I thank you for your attention.

Crisis of Greed

Gabriel Kolko

Gabriel Kolko is the author of the classic Century of War: Politics, Conflicts and Society since 1914 *and, more recently,* Another Century of War? *In Spokesman 91, we featured an extract from his new book* The Age of War *(Lynne Rienner Publishers) which was published earlier this year.*

There has been a profound and fundamental change in the world economy over the past decade. The very triumph of financial liberalisation and deregulation, one of the keystones of the 'Washington consensus' that the US government, International Monetary Fund (IMF), and World Bank have persistently and successfully attempted over the past decades to implement, has also produced a deepening crisis that its advocates scarcely expected.

The global financial structure is today far less transparent than ever. There are many fewer reporting demands imposed on those who operate in it. Financial adventurers are constantly creating new 'products' that defy both nation-states and international banks. The IMF's managing director, Rodrigo de Rato, at the end of May 2006 deplored these new risks – risks that the weakness of the US dollar and its mounting trade deficits have magnified greatly.

De Rato's fears reflect the fact that the IMF has been undergoing both structural and intellectual crises. Structurally, its outstanding credit and loans have declined dramatically since 2003, from over $70 billion to a little over $20 billion today, doubling its available resources and leaving it with far less leverage over the economic policies of developing nations – and even a smaller income than its expensive operations require. It is now in deficit. A large part of its problems is due to the doubling in world prices for all commodities since 2003 – especially petroleum, copper, silver, zinc, nickel, and the like – that the developing nations traditionally export. While there will be fluctuations in this upsurge, there is also reason to think it may endure because rapid economic growth in China, India, and elsewhere has created a burgeoning demand that did not exist before – when the balance-of-trade systematically favoured the rich nations.

The United States has seen its net foreign asset position fall as Japan, emerging Asia, and oil-exporting nations have become far more powerful over the past decade, and they have increasingly become creditors to the US. As the US deficits mount with its imports being far greater than its exports, the value of the dollar has been declining – 28 per cent against the euro from 2001 to 2005 alone.

Even more, the IMF and World Bank were severely chastened by the 1997-2000 financial meltdowns in East Asia, Russia, and elsewhere, and many of its key leaders lost faith in the anarchic premises, descended from classical laissez-faire economic thought, which guided its policy advice until then. '…[O]ur knowledge of economic growth is extremely incomplete,' many in the IMF now admit, and 'more humility' on its part is now warranted. The IMF claims that much has been done to prevent the reoccurrence of another crisis similar to that of 1997-98, but the international economy has changed dramatically since then and, as Stephen Roach of MorganStanley has warned, the world 'has done little to prepare itself for what could well be the next crisis.'

The whole nature of the global financial system has changed radically in ways that have nothing whatsoever to do with 'virtuous' national economic policies that follow IMF advice – ways the IMF cannot control. The investment managers of private equity funds and major banks have displaced national banks and international bodies such as the International Monetery Fund, moving well beyond the existing regulatory structures. In many investment banks, the traders have taken over from traditional bankers because buying and selling shares, bonds, derivatives and the like now generate the greater profits, and taking more and higher risks is now the rule among what was once a fairly conservative branch of finance. They often bet with house money. Low-interest rates have given them and other players throughout the world a mandate to do new things, including a spate of dubious mergers that were once deemed foolhardy. There are also fewer legal clauses to protect investors, so that lenders are less likely than ever to compel mismanaged firms to default. Aware that their bets are increasingly risky, hedge funds are making it much more difficult to withdraw money they play with. Traders have 're-intermediated' themselves between the traditional borrowers – both national and individual – and markets, deregulating the world financial structure and making it far more unpredictable and susceptible of crises. They seek to generate high investment returns – which is the key to their compensation – and they take mounting risks to do so.

In March 2006, the International Monetary Fund released Garry J. Schinasi's book, *Safeguarding Financial Stability*, giving it unusual prominence then and thereafter. Schinasi's book is essentially alarmist, and it both reveals and documents in great and disturbing detail the IMF's deep anxieties. Essentially, 'deregulation and liberalisation,' which the IMF and proponents of the 'Washington consensus' advocated for decades, has become a nightmare. It has created 'tremendous private and social benefits' but it also holds 'the potential (although not necessarily a high likelihood) for fragility, instability, systemic risk, and adverse economic consequences.' Schinasi's superbly documented book confirms his conclusion that the irrational development of global finance, combined with deregulation and liberalisation, has 'created scope for financial innovation and enhanced the mobility of risks.' Schinasi and the International Monetary Fund advocate a radical new framework to monitor and prevent the problems now able to emerge, but success 'may have as much to do with good luck' as policy design and market surveillance. Leaving the future to luck is not what economics originally promised.

The International Monetary Fund is desperate, and it is not alone. As the Argentina financial meltdown proved, countries that do not succumb to IMF and banker pressures can play on divisions within the IMF membership – particularly the US – bankers and others to avoid many, although scarcely all, foreign demands. About $140 billion in sovereign bonds to private creditors and the IMF were at stake, terminating at the end of 2001 as the largest national default in history. In the 1990s, banks were eager to loan Argentina money, and they ultimately paid for it. Since then, however, commodity prices have soared, the growth rate of developing nations in 2004 and 2005 was over double that of high income nations –- a pattern projected to continue through 2008 – and as early as 2003 developing countries were already the source of 37 per cent of the foreign direct investment in other developing nations. China accounts for a great part of this growth, but it also means that the International Monetary Fund and rich bankers of New York, Tokyo, and London have much less leverage than ever.

At the same time, the far greater demand of hedge funds and other investors for risky loans, combined with low interest rates that allow hedge funds to use borrowed money to make increasingly precarious bets, has also led to much higher debt levels as borrowers embark on mergers and other adventures that would otherwise be impossible.

Growing complexity is the order of the world economy that has emerged in the past decade, and the endless negotiations of the World Trade Organisation have failed to overcome the subsidies and protectionism that have thwarted a global free trade agreement and the end of threats of trade wars. Combined, the potential for much greater instability – and greater dangers for the rich – now exists in the entire world economy.

High-speed global economics

The global financial problem that is emerging is tied into an American fiscal and trade deficit that is rising quickly. Since Bush entered office in 2001 he has added over $3 trillion to federal borrowing limits, which are now almost $9 trillion. So long as there is a continued devaluation of the US dollar, banks and financiers will seek to protect their money and risky financial adventures will appear increasingly worthwhile. This is the context, but Washington advocated greater financial liberalisation long before the dollar weakened. This conjunction of factors has created infinitely greater risks than the proponents of the 'Washington consensus' ever believed possible.

There are now many hedge funds, with which we are familiar, but they now deal in credit derivatives – and numerous other financial instruments that have been invented since then, and markets for credit derivative futures are in the offing. The credit derivative market was almost non-existent in 2001, grew fairly slowly until 2004 and then went into the stratosphere, reaching $17.3 trillion by the end of 2005.

What are credit derivatives? *The Financial Times*' chief capital markets writer, Gillian Tett, tried to find out – but failed. About ten years ago, some J.P. Morgan bankers were in Boca Raton, Florida, drinking, throwing each other into the swimming pool, and the like, and they came up with a notion of a new financial instrument that was too complex to be easily copied (financial ideas cannot be copyrighted) and which was sure to make them money. But Tett was highly critical of its potential for causing a chain reaction of losses that will engulf the hedge funds that have leaped into this market. Warren Buffett, second richest man in the world, who knows the financial game as well as anyone, has called credit derivatives 'financial weapons of mass destruction.' Nominally insurance against defaults, they encourage far greater gambles and credit expansion. Enron used them extensively, and it was one secret of their success – and eventual bankruptcy with $100 billion in losses. They are not monitored in any real sense, and two experts called them 'maddeningly opaque.' Many of these innovative financial products, according to one finance director, 'exist in cyberspace' only and often are simply tax dodges for the ultra-rich. It is for reasons such as these, and yet others such as split capital trusts, collateralised debt obligations, and market credit default swaps that are even more opaque, that the International Monetary Fund and financial authorities are so worried.

Banks simply do not understand the chain of exposure and who owns what – senior financial regulators and bankers now admit this. The Long-Term Capital Management hedge fund meltdown in 1998, which involved only about $5 billion in equity, revealed this. The financial structure is now infinitely more complex and far larger – the top 10 hedge funds alone in March 2006 had $157 billion in assets. Hedge funds claim to be honest but those who guide them are compensated for the profits they make, which means taking risks. But there are thousands of hedge funds and many collect inside information, which is technically illegal but it occurs anyway. The system is fraught with dangers, starting with the compensation structure, but it also assumes a constantly rising stock market and much, much else. Many fund managers are incompetent. But the 26 leading hedge fund managers earned an average of $363 million each in 2005; James Simons of Renaissance Technologies earned $1.5 billion.

There is now a consensus that all this, and much else, has created growing dangers. We can put aside the persistence of imbalanced budgets based on spending increases or tax cuts for the wealthy, much less the world's volatile stock and commodity markets which caused hedge funds this last May to show far lower returns than they have in at least a year. It is anyone's guess which way the markets will go, and some will gain while others lose. Hedge funds still make lots of profits, and by the spring of 2006 they were worth about $1.2 trillion worldwide, but they are increasingly dangerous. More than half of them give preferential treatment to certain big investors, and the US Security and Exchange Commission has since mid-June 2006 openly deplored the practice because the panic, if not chaos, potential in such favouritism is now too obvious to ignore. The practice is 'a ticking time bomb,' as one industry lawyer described it. These credit risks – risks that exist in other forms as well – seemed ready to materialise when the *Financial Times*' Tett reported at the end of June that an unnamed investment bank was trying to unload 'several billion dollars' in loans it had made to hedge funds. If true, 'this marks a startling watershed for the financial system.' Bankers had become 'ultracreative... in their efforts to slice, dice and redistribute risk, at this time of easy liquidity.' Low interest rates, Avinash Persaud, one of the gurus of finance concluded, had led investors to use borrowed money to play the markets, and 'a painful deleveraging is as inevitable as night follows day ... The only question is its timing.' There was no way that hedge funds, which had become precociously intricate in seeking safety, could avoid a reckoning and be 'forced to sell their most liquid investments'. 'I will not bet on that happy outcome,' the *Financial Times*' chief expert concluded in surveying some belated attempts to redeem the hedge funds from their own follies.

A great deal of money went from investors in rich nations into emerging market stocks, which have been especially hard-hit in the past weeks, and if they leave then the financial shock will be great — the dangers of a meltdown exist there too.

Problems are structural, such as the greatly increasing corporate debt loads to core earnings, which have grown substantially from four to six times over the past year because there are fewer legal clauses to protect investors from loss –- and keep companies from going bankrupt when they should. So long as interest rates have been low, leveraged loans have been the solution. With hedge funds and other financial instruments, there is now a market for incompetent, debt-ridden firms. The rules some once erroneously associated with capitalism — probity and the like — no longer hold.

Problems are also inherent in speed and complexity, and these are very diverse and almost surreal. Credit derivatives are precarious enough, but at the end of May the International Swaps and Derivatives Association revealed that one in every five deals, many of them involving billions of dollars, involved major errors – as the volume of trade increased, so did errors. They doubled in the period after 2004. Many deals were written on scraps of paper and not properly recorded. 'Unconscionable' was Alan Greenspan's description. He was 'frankly shocked'. Other trading, however, is determined by mathematical algorithm ('volume-weighted average price', it is called) for which PhDs trained in quantitative methods are hired. Efforts to remedy this mess only began in June 2006, and they are very far from resolving a major and accumulated problem that involves stupendous sums.

On 24 April, Stephen Roach, Morgan Stanley's chief economist, wrote that a major financial crisis was in the offing and that the global institutions to forestall it– ranging from the International Monetary Fund and World Bank to other mechanisms of the international financial architecture – were utterly inadequate.

Hong Kong's chief secretary in early June deplored the hedge funds' risks and dangers. The IMF's iconoclastic chief economist, Raghuram Rajan, at the same time warned that the hedge funds' compensation structure encouraged those in charge of them to increasingly take risks, thereby endangering the whole financial system. By late June, Roach was even more pessimistic: 'a certain sense of anarchy' dominated the academic and political communities, and they were 'unable to explain the way the new world is working.' In its place, mystery prevailed. Reality was out of control.

The entire global financial structure is becoming uncontrollable in crucial ways its nominal leaders never expected, and instability is increasingly its hallmark. Financial liberalisation has produced a monster, and resolving the many problems that have emerged is scarcely possible for those who deplore controls on those who seek to make money – whatever means it takes to do so. The Bank for International Settlements' annual report, released 26 June, discusses all these problems and the triumph of predatory economic behaviour and trends 'difficult to rationalise'. The sharks have outfoxed the more conservative bankers. 'Given the complexity of the situation and the limits of our knowledge, it is extremely difficult to predict how all this might unfold.' The Bank does not want its fears to cause a panic, and circumstances compel it to remain on the side of those who are not alarmist. But it now concedes that a big 'bang' in the markets is a possibility, and it sees 'several market-specific reasons for a concern about a degree of disorder'. We are 'currently not in a situation' where a meltdown is likely to occur but 'expecting the best but planning for the worst' is still prudent. For a decade, it admits, global economic trends and 'financial imbalances' have created increasing dangers, and 'understanding how we got to where we are is crucial in choosing policies to reduce current risks'. The Bank for International Settlements is very worried.

Given such profound and widespread pessimism, the vultures from the investment houses and banks have begun to position themselves to profit from the imminent business distress – a crisis they see as a matter of timing rather than principle. Investment banks since the beginning of 2006 have vastly expanded their loans to leveraged buy-outs, pushing commercial banks out of a market they once dominated. To win a greater share of the market, they are making riskier deals and increasing the danger of defaults among highly leveraged firms. There is now a growing consensus among financial analysts that defaults will increase substantially in the very near future. But because there is money to be made, experts in distressed debt and restructuring companies in or near bankruptcy are in greater demand. Goldman Sachs has just hired one of Rothschild's stars in restructuring. All the factors which make for crashes – excessive leveraging, rising interest rates, etc. – exist, and those in the know anticipate that companies in difficulty will be in a much more advanced stage of trouble when investment banks enter the picture. But this time they expect to squeeze hedge funds out of the potential profits because they have more capital to play with.

Contradictions now wrack the world's financial system, and a growing consensus now exists between those who endorse it and those, like myself, who believe the status quo is both crisis-prone as well as immoral. If we are to believe the institutions and personalities who have been in the forefront of the defence of capitalism, and we should, it may very well be on the verge of serious crises.

Whose Century?

Immanuel Wallerstein

Immanuel Wallerstein is the former President of the International Sociological Association (1994-1998), and chair of the international Gulbenkian Commission on the Restructuring of the Social Sciences (1993-1995). He writes in three domains of world-systems analysis: the historical development of the modern world-system; the contemporary crisis of the capitalist world-economy; the structures of knowledge. Books in each of these domains include respectively The Modern World-System *(3 vols.);* Utopistics, or Historical Choices for the Twenty-first Century; *and* Unthinking Social Science: The Limits of Nineteenth-Century Paradigms.

In 1941, Henry Luce proclaimed the twentieth century the American century. And most analysts have agreed with him ever since. Of course, the twentieth century was more than merely the American century. It was the century of the decolonisation of Asia and Africa. It was the century of the flourishing of both fascism and communism as political movements. And it was the century of both the Great Depression and the incredible, unprecedented expansion of the world-economy in the 25 years after the end of the Second World War.

But nonetheless, it was the American century. The United States became the unquestioned hegemonic power in the period 1945-1970 and shaped a world-system to its liking. The United States became the premier economic producer, the dominant political force, and the cultural centre of the world-system. The United States, in short, ran the show, at least for a while.

Now, the United States is in visible decline. More and more analysts are willing to say this openly, even if the official line of the US establishment is to deny this vigorously, just as a certain portion of the world left insists on the continued hegemony of the United States. But clear-minded realists on all sides recognise that the US star is growing dimmer. The question that underlies all serious prognostication is, then, whose century is the twenty-first century?

Of course, it is only 2006, and a bit early to answer this question with any sense of certainty. But nonetheless, political leaders everywhere are making bets on the answer and shaping their policies accordingly. If we rephrase the question to ask merely what may the world look like in, for example, 2025, we may at least be able to say something intelligent.

There are basically three sets of answers to the question of what the world will look like in 2025. The first is that the United States will enjoy one last fling, a revival of power, and will continue to rule the roost in the absence of any serious military contender. The second is that

China will displace the United States as the world's superpower. The third is that the world will become an arena of anarchic and relatively unpredictable multipolar disorder. Let us examine the plausibility of each of these three predictions.

The United States on top? There are three reasons to doubt this. The first, an economic reason, is the fragility of the US dollar as the sole reserve currency in the world economy. The dollar is sustained now by massive infusions of bond purchases by Japan, China, Korea, and other countries. It is highly unlikely that this will continue. When the dollar falls dramatically, it may momentarily increase the sale of manufactured goods, but the United States will lose its command on world wealth and its ability to expand the deficit without serious immediate penalty. The standard of living will fall and there will be an influx of new reserve currencies, including the euro and the yen.

The second reason is military. Both Afghanistan and especially Iraq have demonstrated in the last few years that it is not enough to have airplanes, ships, and bombs. A nation must also have a very large land force to overcome local resistance. The United States does not have such a force, and will not have one, due to internal political reasons. Hence, it is doomed to lose such wars.

The third reason is political. Nations throughout the world are drawing the logical conclusion that they can now defy the United States politically. Take the latest instance: the Shanghai Cooperation Organisation, which brings together Russia, China, and four Central Asian republics, is about to expand to include India, Pakistan, Mongolia, and Iran. Iran has been invited at the very moment that the United States is trying to organise a worldwide campaign against the regime. *The Boston Globe* has called this correctly 'an anti-Bush alliance' and a 'tectonic shift in geopolitics.'

Will China then emerge on top by 2025? To be sure, China is doing quite well economically, is expanding its military force considerably, and is even beginning to play a serious political role in regions far from its borders. China will undoubtedly be much stronger in 2025; however, China faces three problems that it must overcome.

The first problem is internal. China is not politically stabilised. The one-party structure has the force of economic success and nationalist sentiment in its favour. But it faces the discontent of about half of the population that has been left behind, and the discontent of the other half about the limits on their internal political freedom.

China's second problem concerns the world economy. The incredible expansion of consumption in China (along with that of India) will take its toll both on the world's ecology and on the possibilities of capital accumulation. Too many consumers and too many producers will have severe repercussions on worldwide profit levels.

The third problem lies with China's neighbours. Were China to accomplish the reintegration of Taiwan, help arrange the reunification of the Koreas, and come to terms (psychologically and politically) with Japan, there might be an East Asian unified geopolitical structure that could assume a hegemonic position.

All three of these problems can be overcome, but it will not be easy. And the odds that China can overcome these difficulties by 2025 are uncertain.

The last scenario is that of multi-polar anarchy and wild economic fluctuations.

Given the inability of maintaining an old hegemonic power, the difficulty of establishing a new one, and the crisis in worldwide capital accumulation, this third scenario appears the most likely.

Copyright by Immanuel Wallerstein, distributed by Agence Global. For rights and permissions, including translations and posting to non-commercial sites, contact: rights@agenceglobal.com

---

SPOKESMAN BOOKS

A Radical Reader
The Struggle for Change in England 1381-1914
Edited by Christopher Hampton

This major anthology spans 500 years of radical protest from the Peasants' Revolt to the First World War. In the richness and variety of its documentation, it provides an alternative political and social history of England.

'There is something for everybody in Mr Hampton's 600 pages ... A most useful, thought-provoking collection.'
Christopher Hill, *The Guardian*

Price: £18.00 | 624pp | ISBN: 0 85124 725 3

The Levellers and the English Revolution
by H. N. Brailsford - edited by Christopher Hill

'H. N. Brailsford thought of this book not as a mere history, but as a profoundly political study, which would convey a message from him to a younger generation. He himself thought that one of the main achievements of his book was to prove that, at decisive moments in the 17th century English Revolution, the intellectual and political initiative lay with the Levellers ... Without the Leveller initiative the course of English history might have been very different.'
Christopher Hill in his foreword

The Levellers and the English Revolution
by H. N Brailsford
edited by Christopher Hill

Price: £18.00 | 715pp indexed | ISBN: 0 85124 154 9

A History of British Socialism
by Max Beer

Max Beer's History is a classic, not only because it was a brilliant pioneering study, but also because it is still urgently relevant to a new generation of socialists.
Price: £11.95 | 271pp | Fully illustrated | ISBN: 0 85124 408 1

Credit/Debit cards accepted | Spokesman Books (LRB), Russell House, Bulwell Lane, Nottingham, NG6 0BT, England
Tel: **0115 9708318** - Fax: **0115 9420433** - e-mail: **elfeuro@compuserve.com**

www.spokesmanbooks.com

Semper Fou

James Alexander Thom

Following our last number entitled Haditha Ethics – From Iraq to Iran, *James Alexander Thom contacted* The Spokesman *at the suggestion of Kurt Vonnegut, himself a regular contributor. Once a serving Marine, now 'a novelist and historian', Mr Thom resides in Bloomington, Indiana.*

It's more than half a century since I wore the green fatigues, but once a Marine, always a Marine. *Semper Fidelis. Semper Fi.*

What's a faithful old Marine to think about the news that a squad of young ones will be tried for the massacre of two dozen innocent Iraqis in a town called Haditha?

What I think about it is that I'm heartsick that it happened, and I'm mad as hell at the scheming fools who put those Marines and the Iraqi victims in that crazy situation.

'Crazy,' in French, is 'fou'. In Scottish, 'fou' means 'drunk'.

Semper Fou. That's my revised Marine motto. Either *fou* is appropriate. I remember we got drunk any time we could. As for crazy, let me just come out and say it:

To train a sane person to do what a Marine must do, you have to brainwash much of the sanity and the humanity out of him.

You must make him so obedient to authority that he's willing to die on command.

You have to obliterate that key religious commandment: Thou shalt not kill.

You certainly must rid him of most of the teachings of Jesus: Blessed are the meek, the merciful, the peacemakers; turn the other cheek, swear not at all …

By walking on water, Jesus might have been good at amphibious landings, but otherwise he just wasn't US Marine Corps material. Sweet and mild thoughts like his are signs of weakness, and in Marine camps the Lord's name is used mostly in vain. Your comrades need you to be strong and brutal and quick to kill, because their lives depend on it. *Semper Fou.* Gung Ho!

Gung ho is an old Chinese term evoking extreme peer pressure; the Marines shouted it as their early version of Hooah! You don't know what peer pressure is until you've bonded into a squad of Marines. You don't know what trigger-happy is until you've been brainwashed to hate those 'gooks' or 'greasers' or 'ragheads' so much that you could wipe them out as remorselessly as figures in a video game. And you're made to believe that any synonym for Marine – Devil Dog, Jarhead, Leatherneck – evokes terror in any enemy. In other words, you're trained to be a terrorist. (But not against civilians, if you can help it.)

Soon after 9-11, Osama bin Laden's Afghanistan training camps were shown on TV, over and over: his *mujahideen* swarming over obstacle courses, blowing things up, firing assault rifles, marching through hot sand. Just like our boot camp. I thought, those guys would make good Marines. They're brave as lions and brainwashed crazy. If only they believed in Jesus, and spoke English and loved the red, white and blue the way Jesus does, they'd be great Marines. Instead, they dress like Jesus but speak a foreign language and believe in some guy called Mohammed, and hate our flag.

Now, thanks to the wizardry of our Crusader-in-Chief, those terrorists have moved their training facilities to Iraq, where they've got our guys surrounded. The last George who managed a tactic that stupid was George Custer. (Unlike George Bush, Custer led the troops in, instead of sending them.)

After news of the Haditha massacre broke (that is, leaked out from its cover-up), Marine General Peter Pace demurred that it wasn't Marine training that made those Marines murder those civilians.

Respectfully, General, the hell it wasn't!

Put yourself in their boots. There you are, trained to the eyeballs for the madness of war. *Semper Fou*. Trapped in that trashed, gritty Fort Apache burg in the desert. Most of the natives hate you for invading and wrecking their country and kicking in their bedroom doors. In their culture you can't stroll into town and flirt with girls in a bar, as Marines do everywhere else in the world. But every few hours it's your duty to swagger out among the hostiles and remind them who's boss in their country: Dick Cheney.

You know they don't like that, so you're expecting a blast or a bullet at every corner. It's 114 degrees and you're encased in heavy clothes and armour and loaded down with ammo and gear, you haven't had a good night's sleep in six months, and those damned Iraqis aren't a bit grateful for the great gift of Christian capitalist democracy you're trying to bestow upon them. You're frustrated and scared and mad, and your trigger finger is twitchy; this is your third tour of this futile, dirty work, and you feel like a hot grenade with the pin pulled, so God help any hadji who messes with you or your buddies …

Then BAM! Your best friend becomes a one-legged, one-armed fountain of blood right before your eyes, and so you do what you've been trained to do: start killing everybody in sight who isn't a Marine.

If you go berserk, that's bad enough. If you keep on killing methodically in a controlled act of vengeance, that's a massacre, and you must be put on trial for murder.

It's said that the massacre isn't such a big deal over there; the Iraqis say it's just what Americans do. They shrug and point out the tortures and homicides at Abu Ghraib and other military prisons, and the tens of thousands of their people who have been killed in the crossfire since George W. Bush invaded their country.

Months ago, almost unreported in the American mainstream media, there came a study saying that as many as 25 percent of US combat troops over there believe they personally have killed innocent people.

Think of coming home and living the rest of your life with that ghastly belief.

Whether or not that squad of Marines goes on trial for murder, there's another squad-sized group of Americans who should. Their names include Bush, Cheney, Rumsfeld, Rice, Wolfowitz, Feith, Perle, Ledeen, Tenet, etc. Many of them profess to be Christian Soldiers, though they never were personally seen marching off to war. They connived to start an unprovoked war, where real soldiers and Marines have to throw their own bodies and souls into the inferno.

Those high-placed schemers are the ones to go on trial for massacre. They're the ones responsible for the destruction of a country and the death of thousands, and for young American veterans who will hitch along on prosthetic limbs, or wake up quaking from traumatic nightmares the rest of their lives.

That's how one old greybeard ex-Marine feels about it.

Semper Fou.

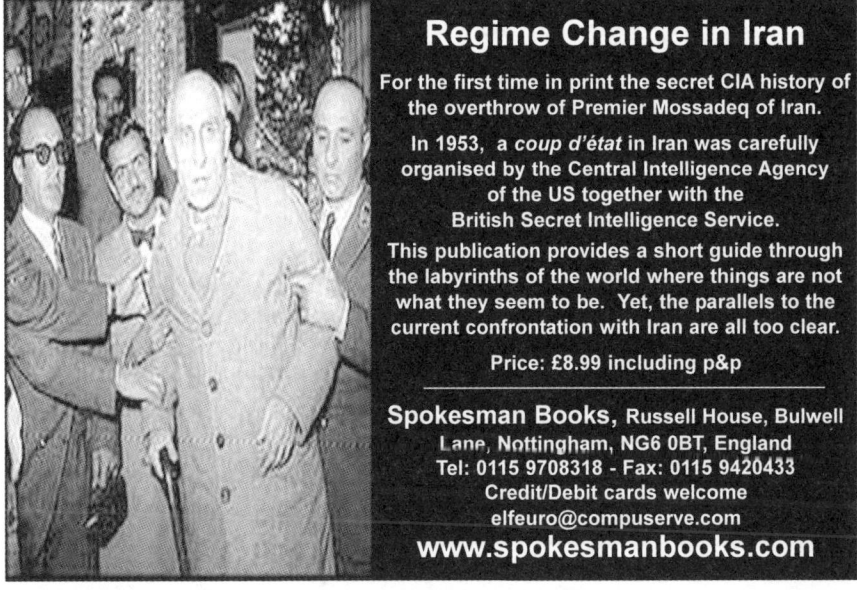

Regime Change in Iran

For the first time in print the secret CIA history of the overthrow of Premier Mossadeq of Iran.

In 1953, a *coup d'état* in Iran was carefully organised by the Central Intelligence Agency of the US together with the British Secret Intelligence Service.

This publication provides a short guide through the labyrinths of the world where things are not what they seem to be. Yet, the parallels to the current confrontation with Iran are all too clear.

Price: £8.99 including p&p

Spokesman Books, Russell House, Bulwell Lane, Nottingham, NG6 0BT, England
Tel: 0115 9708318 - Fax: 0115 9420433
Credit/Debit cards welcome
elfeuro@compuserve.com

www.spokesmanbooks.com

THE BERTRAND RUSSELL PEACE FOUNDATION
DOSSIER

2006   Number 21

LEBANON – TIME TO REBUILD

Hezbollah Secretary-General Hassan Nasrallah spoke on Al-Manar televison on 14 August 2006, the first day of the cease-fire following Israel's recent invasion of Lebanon. These excerpts are taken from his broadcast.

'Peace be upon you. Today is a great day when our people are going back to their homes, back to their villages. I come to you today with a message, and I would like in this message to focus on some of the issues. First, what we are facing today. I don't want to evaluate, and I don't want to talk in details. But I will summarise it in a few words. We are witnessing a strategic and historic victory. This is no exaggeration. This is a victory for Lebanon – all of Lebanon – for the resistance, and for the entire nation.

What is the meaning of this? What is the evidence? This is what I will leave to talk about in the next few days. Because talking about this issue is mainly about the martyrs, the sacrifices of the martyrs, the resistance martyrs, the martyrs from all the parties, all the honourable resistance, from the army, the security forces, the civil defence martyrs, the media martyrs, men, women, civilians who were killed, specially in the massacres, from the first days until yesterday in the southern part of Beirut. Because talking about victory is talking about the resistors, the sacrifice, steadfastness, strength, people, family, beloved ones, friends, patience, confidence, strong will, and the loyal ones who stood with us in Lebanon, and outside of Lebanon during all this war ...

I would like to talk about the displaced refugees and the return to their homes, and what's after the return. Of course, in the first place, I would like to greet those who stood strong, confronting the enemy. It was an unbearable burden because the bombardment from the air, the sea, and the land was not paralleled before in the history of Lebanon. The amount of destruction by the Israeli enemy is unsurpassed. Not just the infrastructure, but also the homes. It's unsurpassed in any war between Israel and Lebanon. There is huge destruction left by this enemy to show us his savagery.

During the last few days they destroyed thousands of homes in the south, in south Beirut, in the Beka Valley, and all over Lebanon. But there was a specific focus on the area in the south of Lebanon, and Beirut's southern suburb. Of course, the goal is to hurt the people, punish the people for their position, their honour, their discipline, their faith, their humanity, and their pride.

Thanks should also be given to those who suffered during the displacement and became refugees, and today they are coming back to their homes, even though they are demolished. I would like to thank the people in the areas, the religious sects, and the country and the government, and all the humanitarian organisations. Everybody who embraced those displaced ones during this difficult war period. I would like to talk to those who are coming back to their homes and to those who never left their homes, about the homes that were destroyed.

There are two types of destruction. I would like to talk about the residential units and homes. Any other destruction such as infrastructure, the economy, and other things that were destroyed, I will postpone talking about until later. Now, the urgent issue is the homes and residential units, because this is where these families live.

For those homes that were hit but are still inhabitable, starting tomorrow morning, the brothers in the cities, villages, and towns will walk around, evaluate, talk to the owners to give immediate financial support to start rebuilding these homes and units as soon as possible.

As for the homes that were completely demolished, and this is the more difficult issue, I would like to tell these families not to worry. What I said at the beginning of the war was not simply meant to boost your steadfastness. Today is the day when I fulfil my promise to you. You don't need to ask anybody for money. You don't need to stand in any line. You don't need to go anywhere for help. My brothers, who are your brothers, are in all villages and cities, and they will come to help you, starting tomorrow morning.

We will co-operate with you. We will help you. We cannot wait for the government, and the government red tape, because it might need some time. What the government can do, we can follow up, co-ordinate with, and be parallel to. We can co-operate together on two lines at the same time, starting tomorrow. The first line is to secure a specific amount of money, a reasonable amount to each family, to help them to rent a home for a full year, and to buy reasonable, suitable furniture for that house. Because rebuilding the homes that were completely destroyed will certainly take several months, and the natural replacement is for these people to rent a home to live in and to buy furniture for this house. That can start tomorrow.

Within a few days, we will be able to cover these cases, even though it is a large number. Until now, the initial statistics regarding destruction of homes and units completely demolished is more than 15,000. I know this is a large number, but we have the will and capability to carry out this rebuilding.

The second parallel line is to remove the debris and start rebuilding, hoping that you together with us, within a few months, that we can rebuild these homes that were destroyed. It's will power, not just money. It's patience, seriousness, hard work, accuracy. These are the values that enabled us to face the attack and achieve victory. With the same values, these feelings and emotions, we can go through the rebuilding phase and also achieve victory in it.

In this regard, I call on all the engineers in our areas, not just the money. It's not enough. We need solidarity, initiative and co-operation on the part of engineers and from the retailers who are selling building supplies and furniture. In other words, you cannot increase your prices because of high demand. They need to be more responsible, more humanitarian, more in a nationalistic way. Don't increase prices.

We also need labour, simple labour, to be able to rebuild on that scale. We might not have enough physical labour because of the situation the country lived through in the last few months. So we all have to volunteer and help those owners to rebuild their homes. I call all the Lebanese youth to volunteer in the same nationalistic spirit that we saw during the war, hosting the displaced ones, civil defence, and zeal for your own country. But specifically I talk to the youth of Hezbollah, all over the country, to the *mujahideen*, to the students, to the union people, to the freelancers. Everybody, we need to converge and start rebuilding in every village, in every city, in every district.

Let's set aside our personal feelings and give as much as we can to rebuild. Even the simple labour we need to help with. We need to be available, and I think that with the large numbers we represent, that we express on their behalf, if every brother would take one or two days, or several days, or a few hours every day, we will be able to make great efforts and help.

This is a great effort and great undertaking. I also call on those who can donate, especially the Lebanese overseas, that we rely on them all the time. Now the door is open. Please help and support us financially because completing the victory only happens after rebuilding, especially homes, even better than before they were demolished. So those honourable families can go back and live in them.

The last topic in this message of mine has to do with the controversy that began a few days ago about disarming Hezbollah and the weapons of Hezbollah. I don't like to go into this part of the argument, but I want this discussion to be responsible and careful.

Dear Brothers, when the war was going on, and the beloved ones of the resistance were writing the books in sacrifice and conducting miracles, there was discussion behind closed doors about the nature of things after the war south of the Litani, about the deployment of the Lebanese army, and the borders, and the international forces, and if this deployment took place, what is the place of the resistance, how will the resistance act about their arms. All these were very responsible discussions. It was always conducted through President Nabih Berri, who represents in reality great Lebanese credibility, and I urge those engaged in this discussion, in the media, to listen to him, and to listen to his voice and to his wisdom in treating this very sensitive issue. All these discussions were taking place before the resolution of the United Nations and after the resolution. Till the last session of the government, this issue was given for discussion. We were surprised that some ministers in the government leaked the discussion and the disagreement to the media, to some of the local Arabic TV channels, and thus the discussion began to grow more and more and went out of control. What was supposed to have been a discussion behind closed doors became a public debate throughout the whole nation, and this, in my opinion, does not serve the best interest of Lebanon, and is not suitable at this time. In any event, I reiterate my call to restore this debate to its official channels ... I would like to say that during this serious discussion and dialogue, and through the wise personalities in this country, and away from the media and the exaggerations, I'm confident that we can reach a suitable solution that takes care of the national interest ...'

RETURN OF 'SON OF STAR WARS'

Tom Baldwin reports in The Times *that the Pentagon is once again actively considering the possibility that Britain might be drawn into the American missile defence system, which became widely known as 'Son of Star Wars'.*

Apparently, British officials have reported that discreet questions are being asked by military planners in the United States: will the Brits accept the ten interceptor units, designed to 'knock out a ballistic missile fired by terrorists or states such as Iran before it reaches the United States'? But the interceptors are not designed to offer such protection to their British hosts, and they are only being offered to London because the Pentagon has now been rejected by Poland and the Czech Republic, which were the preferred sites.

The Americans have ruled out a sideways shift in Central Europe, because the Hungarians are 'too close to Russia'. The Russians are understandably unenthusiastic about an American military presence in Central Europe, although until recently this lack of enthusiasm would be seen by right-wing leaders in Poland or the Czech Republic as a modest plus. Today, the downside of this commitment is evidently more apparent, as the post-Cold War thaw between East and West is being heated up by engagements in the Middle East.

The justification of the Son of Star Wars by reference to Iran is itself a case in point. There is not a very live prospect of Iranian missile attacks on the United States, and the only power which might consider such attacks for the foreseeable future remains Russia. But the mock *détente* forbids the unfriendly reference to Russia, and requires the nomination of an alternative bogey. That the alternative has no nuclear missiles, and is unlikely to have any for a very long time, if at all, is no impediment to the spin machines of the American military. How malleable will the British prove to be in this respect?

'The US State Department is investigating whether Israel's use of American-made cluster bombs in southern Lebanon violated secret agreements with the United States that restrict when it can employ such weapons, two officials said ... The investigation by the department's Office of Defense Trade Controls began this week after reports that three types of American cluster munitions, anti-personnel weapons that spray bomblets over a wide area, have been found in many areas of southern Lebanon and were responsible for civilian casualties.' (*New York Times*, 24 August 2006)

Reviews

Failed Superstate

Noam Chomsky, *Failed States: The Abuse of Power and the Assault on Democracy*, Hamish Hamilton, 2006, 306 pages, hardback ISBN 9780241143230, £16.99

Noam Chomsky's latest book deliberately refers to the United States as 'Failed States', the opprobrium which US governments apply to their enemies which they say lack the democracy the United States prides itself on supposedly possessing. This is not an anti-American book. On every one of the claims made by US governments for their policies, which Chomsky examines with meticulous attention to the appropriate references, he can show that the opinions of the American people are overwhelmingly opposed to their governments' policies.

On the main issues of US policy which Chomsky examines, the policies are shown not only to be contrary to the accepted laws of nations and to democratic principles, quite at odds with the grand rhetoric with which they are proclaimed, but also to be seriously destructive of the security and comfort of the American people themselves. The cases he cites begin with the so-called 'war on terror' in which US governments and their allies, and notably Blair's Britain, are revealed as the real terrorists. US governments have a long history of terrorising peoples – from the indigenous American Indians, to Latin America and across the world to Hiroshima, Vietnam and Iraq. The threat of first use of nuclear weapons is the ultimate terrorism encompassing the prospect of destroying all life on the planet.

The US governments' concept of outlaw states is Chomsky's second case. The outlaws are supposedly those like North Korea, Iraq or Iran which, under leaders not approved of by the United States, should not be allowed nuclear weapons. The real outlaw (out-law) is, of course, the United States which excludes itself from the rulings of the United Nations, the Non-Proliferation Treaty, the International Court of Justice, the Kyoto Protocols, and even the UN Convention against Torture, which the US Senate signed but with its own interpretation of 'torture', repeated by Secretary Rice in her justification of the abominable practice of 'rendition' of prisoners to countries where abuse is the norm. The extension to actual military aggression of this principle of US exclusion from international law provides Chomsky's third case. Thus, the bombing of Serbia including Belgrade without UN sanction could be called 'illegal but legitimate', as Chomsky revealed in his earlier books on the Balkan wars, *New Military Humanism* and *A New Generation Draws the Line*. Unfortunately, many on the political left decided on humanitarian grounds to condone this bombing although, as Chomsky demonstrates, the humanitarian disaster in Kosovo took place after and not before the bombs fell.

Promotion of democracy abroad is the boast of George W. Bush's military adventures. There is nothing new in this justification for military action outside the United States, as Chomsky shows at some length in citing US intervention throughout Central and South America and in Vietnam, long before the current incursions into the Middle East, Afghanistan, the Balkans and western Asia. This was the theme of earlier US historians, William and Mary Beard, and more recently of Andrew Bacevich. Behind the democratic rhetoric Chomsky can easily show that today as ever the real rationale is control over raw materials and most particularly over oil and gas, the reserves, the production and transport. Chomsky reminds us that the British Empire with its civilising claims, most recently lauded by its latest apologist, Niall Ferguson, was not different in its treatment of native peoples. Chomsky quotes the astonishing orders of Churchill in May 1945 to draw up war plans for 'Operation Unthinkable' having no less an aim than 'the elimination of Russia'. Where democracy produces results unacceptable to US governments, as in the case of the victories of Sukarno in Indonesia, Mossadeq in Iran, Allende in Chile, Chavez in Venezuela, or Hamas in Palestine, there is no hesitation on the part of US governments to refuse recognition or seek forcefully to overthrow these democrats.

US policy in the Middle East, indeed, and most particularly the cases of Lebanon, Egypt and Palestine, supplies Chomsky with the strongest supporting evidence for his onslaught against the sincerity of US governments' claims to a Messianic mission abroad. The most recent Israeli invasion of Lebanon has taken place since Chomsky published his latest book, but he has no difficulty in showing that Israeli governments, fully supported by the United States, had no intention after 1973 of accepting a Palestinian state or reaching a peaceful settlement with the surrounding Arab states.

Chomsky argues convincingly that the Camp David proposals, claimed by Clinton to be a fair settlement which Arafat walked away from, never had any chance of being accepted by any Palestinian leader including Bush's nominee, Mahmoud Abbas. Egypt won US favour by its support for the US actions in launching the first Gulf War, but the dictatorship of Hosni Mubarak can hardly be claimed as a democracy. Chomsky ends this chapter by quoting from a Pentagon advisory panel, the Defense Science Board, which concluded in December 2004 that 'Muslims do not "hate our freedom", but rather they hate our policies'. As Muslims see it, the Report continues, 'American occupation of Afghanistan and Iraq has not led to democracy there, but only more chaos and suffering'. George W. Bush, Chomsky concludes, has become bin Laden's best ally in resisting a true development of democracy in Saudi Arabia.

Chomsky's last chapter reviews the progress of 'Democracy Promotion at Home'. It is not difficult for him to assess the results of the last two Presidential elections as a travesty of democracy. More serious is the evidence he adduces not only for the growth of inequality in the United States in the last four decades, but also for the widening gap there between Government policies and public opinion as revealed in opinion polls. This applies not only to foreign policy, but also more especially to policies for education and provision for health and social security. Decline of economic growth is matched by even greater decline in educational and health standards. The Bush administration can be seen as steadily chipping away at standards that had been slowly and painfully won over the years and particularly in the Roosevelt era.

Chomsky added an Afterword to the book before its publication in 2006. In this he underlines the absolute failure of US policies in Iraq and refers to the challenge to US policies presented by the new regimes appearing in Latin America. He gives the amusing story of the Venezuelan state oil company offering to provide low cost oil to low income residents of Boston and later elsewhere in the US, President Chavez hoping that 'the deal would present a friendly challenge to US oil companies ... to use their windfall profits to help poor families survive the winter'. To end the Afterword, Chomsky offers a brief summary of 'a few simple suggestions' for the United States:

'(1) accept the jurisdiction of the International Criminal Court and the World Court; (2) sign and carry forward the Kyoto protocols; (3) let the UN take the lead in international crises; (4) rely on diplomatic and economic measures rather than military ones in confronting terror; (5) keep to the traditional interpretation of the UN Charter; (6) give up the Security Council veto and "have a decent respect for the opinion of mankind" as the Declaration of Independence advises, even if power centres disagree; (7) cut back sharply on military spending and sharply increase social spending.'

'As always in the past', Chomsky concludes, 'the tasks require dedicated day by day engagement to create – in part re-create – the basis for a functioning democratic culture, in which the public plays some role in determining policies, not only in the political arena, from which it is largely excluded, but also in the crucial economic arena, from which it is excluded in principle.'

Michael Barratt Brown

Lord of Mistrust

Steven Kettel, *Dirty Politics? New Labour, British Democracy and the Invasion of Iraq,* **Zed Books, 213 pages, hardback ISBN 1842777408 £55, paperback ISBN 1842777416 £14.99**

When Tony Blair finally leaves office as Prime Minister, whether by his own decision or by public and parliamentary pressure, he will depart with an unenviable reputation. Much of it will be due to his role in the war on Iraq. This book explains why he has lost support.

The Prime Minister is now mistrusted by a substantial section of the electorate. Until comparatively recently Labour's lead in opinion polls reflected even greater disenchantment with the Tories than with New Labour. Today that appears to have changed.

Tony Blair is regarded as the political leader who took Britain into an aggressive war in support of the United States. The war has been costly both in lives and resources. It was based upon false information and was in defiance of the Charter of the United Nations. It is seen as the symbol of the servility of the

British Government towards the ambition of the ruling circles of the United States to exercise dominating influence in many areas of the world. The war has not brought peace to the Middle East. The killings continue.

In the eyes of the majority of the British public the war on Iraq and the refusal of Tony Blair to give support for an earlier cease-fire in the Lebanon have not diminished the threat of terrorism. On the contrary, the policies of the United States and Britain have contributed to the recruitment of a small minority group prepared to kill others and to kill themselves by terrorist acts.

For anyone wanting to trace the sequence of events leading to this outcome, there is unlikely to be a better or more concise guide than this book by Steven Kettel. The author is a lecturer in the Department of Politics and International Studies at the University of Warwick. He combines a scholarly style of writing with a strong commitment to speak the truth as he has found it. His narrative is thoroughly referenced and documented and, though he expresses his point of view with clarity and sharpness, he seeks also to explain the standpoint of the Government and its principal supporters.

All the essential events leading to the present state of public opinion in Britain concerning the Iraq war are covered in the book. There was the claim that Iraq had weapons of mass destruction and that these weapons were in a state of readiness, representing an imminent threat to British security. It proved to be false. There was the argument about the legality under international law of an attack on Iraq without a so-called 'second resolution' from the Security Council. Such a resolution was not carried. The Secretary-General of the United Nations made it clear that the subsequent assault on Iraq did not have UN authority.

There were rumblings of opposition both within the Parliamentary Labour Party and in the Cabinet. Robin Cook, and eventually Clare Short, resigned from the Cabinet. At one stage 139 Labour MPs voted in favour of a parliamentary amendment stating that the case for war had yet to be made. The anti-war movement in Britain succeeded in mobilising the biggest street protest demonstration in British history.

There was also the tragic death of Dr David Kelly, the security official who it was said had misgivings about the 'evidence' in the Government's case for war. Related to it were the circumstances surrounding the departure of Andrew Gilligan from the BBC and the resignations of Gavyn Davies from the Chairmanship of the BBC and Greg Dyke as Director-General. All three had been the subject of attack for their part in reporting or permitting broadcasts on the war which the Government regarded as too critical and one-sided. Alastair Campbell, the press spokesman for the Prime Minister, was deeply involved in the criticism of the BBC.

This book is not, however, only about the Iraq war. The author is concerned about the wider political implications of the clear divergence between the policy of the Government and the predominant critical mood of the public. To put it briefly: how is it possible for the Government to continue for so long with a policy that most of the electorate do not support? What does this tell us about the state of democracy in Britain?

The conventional reply to this question is that the present Government has a substantial parliamentary majority and its mandate was re-affirmed in a General Election as recently as the year 2005. Moreover, the Government sought and secured Parliamentary approval for the war and the principal Opposition party supported the invasion of Iraq. The Prime Minister, it is argued, is therefore justified in giving strong leadership in support of a cause which he believes to be of world importance, even though it has brought for the time being some unpopularity.

The author of this book maintains that it is the centralised, hierarchical and élitist underpinnings of the British political system that have provided the possibility for the pursuit of the Iraq war policy. This underpinning of centralised, hierarchical and élitist control has been further developed and implemented by senior figures within the New Labour leadership. They have succeeded up to now because, in the words of the author of this book, '… it reveals not so much the failure of British democracy, as that it signifies the triumph of its essentially undemocratic underlying norms and values'.

The inner group of the New Labour leadership have not only taken full advantage and even developed certain undemocratic features of British constitutional arrangements, such as, for example, the power of patronage belonging to the Prime Minister and wide-ranging unilateral powers exercised in the name of the sovereign, but they have also brought about changes in the structure of the labour movement to consolidate their power.

New Labour has diminished the collective influence of the Cabinet, diminished the influence of the National Executive of the Party, changed the role of the Party conference, and has largely succeeded in curbing opposition from the unions. Even the chairmanship of the Party nationally has been transformed into an instrument of patronage.

The other side of this coin is that Party membership has slumped and Party activity at local level has declined steeply. The author points out that favourable election results are not as convincing as they might appear at first sight.

At the last General Election Labour was elected with a substantial majority of seats, even though only 21.6% of those entitled to vote cast their votes for Labour candidates. In England Labour won far more seats than the Conservatives even though the Conservatives polled more votes than Labour. At the next General Election there will be some redistribution of constituencies to take account of population changes.

In the final chapter of this book the author puts forward suggestions for a reform agenda. They affect both policy and the structure of representative democracy. He urges that 'the stultifying edifice of the Party system' should be tackled, and that the 'dominant notion of representation' should be dislodged and replaced with 'one based on a more delegatory conception'. He suggests also that reform measures might include secret voting in Parliament for MPs, more frequent general elections, staggered elections for a second chamber, the resolution of specific issues by national referenda and the introduction of mechanisms for the public to recall and remove representatives from office between elections on grounds of poor performance.

Among the author's other suggestions for reform are that there should be a codified constitution, a Bill of Rights, greater powers for Parliament, more checks and balances on executive power, a more rigorous relationship between the political and the intelligence spheres of the British state, a strengthening of the committee system, dilution of prerogative powers, more formalised relations between ministers, civil servants and special advisors and some form of proportional representation.

The adoption of some of these suggestions would be helpful. Not all, however, would find support in the labour movement.

The key surely lies within the labour movement itself. And within the labour movement the most important contributor for change should be the unions. It is they, with their day-to-day contact with the problems facing working people, that should be the long-term guarantee that the Labour Party will not depart from – and, indeed will defend and further — the interests of working people, their dependants, pensioners, the disabled, and the self-employed.

It is within the potential influence of the unions to change the course of the Labour Party from so-called New Labour to the traditional aims and values of the labour movement. To do this, however, they must be prepared to 'punch their weight' within the Party. This is necessary at all levels, including the Party conference, the National Executive, the local constituencies, and within the selection procedure for candidates. Their initiative would be welcomed by many constituency activists.

This is a good book, particularly on the Iraq war. It is likely to serve as a very helpful source of reference. Its exposure of some of the deficiencies of the British political system is thoughtful and stimulating, but its suggestions for change, in the view of this reviewer, are not always on target.

J.E. Mortimer

Unsustainable War

Westmorland General Meeting of the Religious Society of Friends, (Quakers), *Preparing for Peace,* **267 pages, paperback ISBN 095505270X £6-99 from PfP, 4 Beetham House, Milnthorpe, Cumbria LA7 &AP, England**

In 2005, Westmorland General Meeting of the Quakers published the book *Preparing for Peace* having asked several international experts, civil and military, to analyse war. They included Dame Margaret Anstee, former UN Under-Secretary General, General Sir Hugh Beach, former Master General of the Ordnance, Judge Richard Goldstone, former Chief Prosecutor, UN International Tribunals, the late Sir Joseph Rotblat, Nobel Peace Prize 1995, Sir Crispin Tickell, former UK Ambassador to the UN, and Brian Walker, former Director General of Oxfam

The project which led to the book began in 2002 when the United States and Britain were already bombing Iraq and, as we now know, preparing to invade. None of the experts consulted found it easy to envisage that all the conditions for a 'just war' could be satisfied, particularly since bombardment, the preferred option, made civilian casualties inevitable. Most of the experts concurred that war as a future tool of foreign policy was also likely to be unsustainable, unsuccessful and damaging – putting at risk even life on earth with a revived proliferation of nuclear weapons.

The invasion of one country by another has been described, I think by John Pilger, as the abuse of human rights that subsumes all other abuses. For an invader to kill and injure people, destroy infrastructures such as those for water supply, sanitation and power supplies, seize assets and privatise them at will, torture and imprison indefinitely without trial those who resist, and devise laws to 'legitimise' all that is imposed without consent, leaves no human right unviolated. That the number of consequent deaths, perhaps over 200,000 people, mainly civilians, is an *estimate* is the final indictment. The invaders of Iraq, the coalition partners of *Operation Iraqi Freedom,* chose not to count the victims.

The book was timely in its anticipation of the Iraq invasion. Its conclusions are strongly vindicated by subsequent events. The authors' recommendations include the strengthening of international law, the removal of immunity, support for the United Nations, an education programme, regulation of the arms trade, and reduced spending on weapons – changes that will allow greater commitment to trade justice and the development of deprived countries.

Few people now doubt that the war was illegal. Two million people in the United Kingdom took to the streets to object at the time. Now we know that the Cabinet and Parliament were misled, that there were two 'dodgy dossiers', that service chiefs demanded assurances from the Attorney General whose advice, not yet fully disclosed, lacks conviction, and that an attempt to secure the authority of the UN for the invasion was not even attempted because there was no prospect of its success. The list of those who insist that the war is illegal include members of both Houses of Parliament, US Senators and Congressmen, the Secretary General of the UN, the Archbishop of Canterbury and General Sir Michael Rose, former head of Nato operations in Bosnia, who demanded the impeachment of Tony Blair in January this year.

A motion for the impeachment of the Prime Minister was drafted some time ago by Adam Price, Plaid Cymru MP for Carmarthen East, and remains with the Speaker of the House of Commons. It may not succeed to impeachment but it should at least lead to debate and inquiry.

Will the United States continue to train 2,500 nuclear warheads on city and other targets none of which is an enemy or a plausible threat? Some of those bases are in the United Kingdom. Will our government go on to spend £25billion on an updated Trident weapons system? Gordon Brown has spoken in favour of that ahead of any debate. As yet we have no assurance that Parliament will be allowed to decide.

Christopher Gifford

The Nuclear Non-Option

Christopher Gifford, *Nuclear Reactors: Do we need more?* **Spokesman for Socialist Renewal, 32 pages, ISBN 0851247261, £2**

To the legacy of ruin which Blair's New Labour government has bequeathed to the British people, in an unwinnable war, destruction of the Health Service, the dividing up of comprehensive education, privatisation of all public services, the last touch is now being added in the dangerously wasteful folly of nuclear arms for a new fleet of Trident submarines and the proliferation of nuclear power stations. Christopher Gifford, who had a long and distinguished career as a Health and Safety Inspector of mines and was involved with the Nuclear Installations Inspectorate on human factors in high risk industries following the Chernobyl disaster, has now written a timely pamphlet to warn us of the dangers of installing more nuclear reactors.

Gifford writes in response to the conversion of the one-time green environmentalist, Sir James Lovelock, author of the Gaia hypothesis (that the planet has evolved as a self-regulating system), to support for the nuclear option as the only way to meet the world's needs for power, without increasing global warming from carbon dioxide emissions to a catastrophic level. Gifford takes on the case of the nuclear lobby step by step. Lovelock's claim that the Sellafield nuclear waste disposal installation was 'clean and tidy' was denied in the reports of the Nuclear Installations Inspectorate. The idea of 'Atoms for Peace' has been rubbished by the evidence of the Central Electricity Generating Board's own chairmen, Lords Hilton and Marshall, to the effect that plutonium from the CEGB's reactors did go into the defence stockpile. And there is the continued underestimate of the true results of the Chernobyl disaster – when the assumption of at least 300,000 deaths and nine million people affected is accepted by Kofi Annan for the United Nations

The assumption that there was no risk from terrorist attack has been ridiculed by the events of 9/11, but the government has taken no steps as required by European Directives to make plans and prepare information for all households in the United Kingdom in the event of a nuclear disaster. The idea that nuclear power is economic depends on whether owners and managers of capital can be convinced that there is a likely profitable return in the near future from their investment. This can only be sustained if the actual costs of decommissioning reactors, estimated by the Department of Trade and Industry at £55bn., are omitted, or promised by government to be covered by subsidies. As for the disposal of nuclear waste, some 10,000 tonnes of this are stored in the United

Kingdom awaiting decision on its long-term future, which the Nuclear Installations Inspectorate regards as unlikely to be safely effected by 2015, especially if the business is privatised. Depleted uranium as a product of the reprocessing of spent fuel from nuclear reactors is now used for increasing the penetrating power of shells – 2000 tonnes of it in the 2003 attack on Iraq, a small part of the million tonnes held world-wide – has undoubted toxic effects on human beings and on the wider environment. These effects can last for thousands of years with many generations affected.

So what are the alternatives? Gifford argues that renewable energy – tidal, hydro, solar, wind, geo-thermal and bio-mass are not only available to fill the gap left by oil and gas, but could be introduced sooner than nuclear, and, he might have added, are more likely to find willing investors. Gifford ends his argument by urging that all plans for new nuclear reactors should be subject to the most rigorous open public inquiries, and no fast tracking for licensing to private contractors with government guarantees.

Michael Barratt Brown

The Essential Saladin

Sir Hamilton Gibb, *The Life of Saladin*, Saqi Essentials, 94 pages, paperback ISBN: 0863569285 £9.99

Saqi Essentials have republished Sir Hamilton Gibb's *The Life of Saladin* in an attractive new edition, recently printed in the Lebanon. The book is prefaced by a short essay from Robert Irwin, which sets out in summary the life of Gibb, and stresses the influence upon him of Ibn Khaldun, the fourteenth century sociologist and historian, whose *Muqaddima* has also recently been republished in an accessible format in English. He points up the debt that Gibb owes to Ibn Khaldun in this work, which is directly based on the works of Baha'ad-Din ibn Shaddad and Imad ad-Din al-Isfahani. Their combined portrait of Saladin is summarised:

> 'Neither warrior nor governor by training or inclination, he it was who inspired and gathered round himself all the elements and forces making for the unity of Islam against the invaders. And this he did, not so much by the example of his personal courage and resolution – which were undeniable – as by his unselfishness, his humility and generosity, his moral vindication of Islam against both its enemies and its professed adherents. He was no simpleton, but for all that an utterly simple and transparently honest man. He baffled his enemies, internal and external, because they expected to find him animated by the same motives as they were, and playing the political game as they played it. Guileless himself, he never expected and seldom understood guile in others – a weakness of which his own family and others took advantage, but only (as a general rule) to come up at the end against his single-minded devotion, which nobody and nothing could bend, to the service of his ideals.'

Irwin's foreword offers much more detail about the sources of this little book, as Gibb says:

'The life and achievements of Saladin constitute one of the great moments in the history of the Crusades. In literature he appears most frequently as a conquering hero, who fought his enemies victoriously and in the end beat them to a standstill. But closer examination of his actual life reveals him not only as a conqueror, but as a man who struggled with enemies of his own side ...'

Modern wars will revive interest in Saladin the warrior, whose exploits are certainly recorded here. But Gibb is also at pains to explain why it was that Saladin inspired one of those who knew him to say: 'This was the only instance of a King's death that was truly mourned by the people'.

Jim Thomas

A Voice of Ireland

Robert W. White, *Ruairí Ó Brádaigh: The Life and Politics of an Irish Revolutionary,* **Indiana University Press, 412 pages, ISBN 0253347084, £18.99**

This year is the 90th anniversary of the 1916 Rising. Ken Loach's film, *The Wind That Shakes The Barley*, which covers the Irish War of Independence against British imperialism, wins the Palme d'Or, and it is the 25th anniversary of the Hunger Strike. It's a good year to read this book.

Ruairí Ó Brádaigh has played a central role in Irish Republicanism from the 1950s, and for those who seek to understand the nature of that tradition it is in the 'must read' category.

In 1918, Republicans contested the British general election and won a democratic majority in favour of an Irish Republic, as a consequence of 1916 and their opposition to the Imperialist War of 1914-18. They abstained from the Westminster Parliament. In January 1919, they formed an all-Ireland Assembly, Dáil Éireann, and its army went to war with the British army of occupation. In the early1920s, Dáil Éireann agreed to a treaty with Britain, which left six counties of Ireland under the control of the British Empire. Those that led the case for accepting a treaty which fell far short of the Republic did so because they believed it provided a stepping stone towards it. Those that did not, extended the idea of abstention from Westminster to the newly established Stormont Assembly in the six counties, and the now 26 county Dáil Éireann. Since the 1920s, wave after wave of Irish Republicans, Fianna Fáil, Clan na Poblachta, Official Sinn Féin and Sinn Féin decided to abandon abstentionism and enter the assemblies established in Ireland.

Ruairí Ó Brádaigh, however, stayed absolutely committed to abstaining, even if elected to the Dáil as he was in 1957 as a candidate for Sinn Féin. As far as Ó Brádaigh was concerned, the Republic, having been established, cannot be disestablished. The elected members of the Dáil that did not take their seats were the real government and the IRA that agreed was the only legitimate army. By the 1950s, the IRA had rebuilt its organisation and felt strong enough to launch a war against the British Empire. They had a level of popular support. In 1955, in the six counties 152,000 people voted for Sinn Féin, electing two MPs and, in 1957, Sinn Féin got 65,640 votes, electing four members of the 26 county Dáil. It was not enough, and even that level of support fell to 36,393 votes in 1961, and Ó Brádaigh and the others lost their seats in the Dáil. In comparison, Fianna Fáil got 512,00 votes in the 1961 election.

A new leadership took over Sinn Féin and, in the late 1960s, it decided to end abstentionism. Sinn Féin's leaders advocated support for a civil rights campaign and a reformed Stormont. They did not believe Ireland was on the verge of a revolution or that the British intended to withdraw. Ó Brádaigh disagreed, led the establishment of Provisional Sinn Féin, and supported the Provisional IRA in its war to obtain a declaration of intent to withdraw. He played a leading role in the negotiations with the British in the 1970s, and developed the concept of a decentralised four Province Ireland, *Eire Nua*, in an effort to allay the concerns of the Unionists after withdrawal. By the 1980s, a new leadership dominated by people from the six counties gained control of Sinn Féin and rejected the *Eire Nua* policy and, in 1986, abstentionism. Ó Brádaigh left and formed Republican Sinn Féin that maintained the policy of abstensionism.

There can be no doubt that Ó Brádaigh is part of a deeply rooted Republican tradition. Every effort to break that tradition, through special courts, internment, torture, and collusion with loyalist terrorists, failed. Republicans are not criminals, and as we mark the 25th anniversary of the Hunger Strike we should remember the strength of will of those Republicans that died seeking political status.

However, the key issue for Ó Brádaigh is that, by participation in the existing structures, Republicans eventually become corrupted, while other Republicans believe armed struggle without popular support will fail. There is evidence for Ó Brádaigh. Fianna Fáil now supports an imperialist war for oil, and Fine Gael are totally opposed to Irish Neutrality. Yet power derives from the people, and a Republic established without their support would have no legitimacy. A Republic has not been established with a ballot box in one hand and an armalite in the other. The decisive majority of Republicans now advocate building the Republic, as initially advocated by Desmond Greaves, by way of a reformed Stormont as part of reconciliation with the Unionists.

However, for the first time since the 1914-18 War, the political élite throughout Ireland is supporting an imperialist war, and the involvement of Irish soldiers in the European Union Battle Groups. If the latest wave of Republicans, led by Adams, go into coalition with Fianna Fáil and support the war and a militarised European Union, then the Republican beliefs of Ó Brádaigh, as happened so many times in Irish history, will be reborn. It is no accident that the phoenix is the symbol of Irish Republicanism, the unyielding enemy of British imperialism.

Roger Cole
Chair, Peace & Neutrality Alliance, www.pana.ie